Eve

HOW TO SATISFY A WOMAN EVERY TIME...

and have her beg for more!

by

NAURA HAYDEN

Bibli O'Phile Books, Inc.
New York, New York

Distributed by Penguin Putnam, Inc.

Published by Bibli O'Phile Books,
200 West 58th Street , Suite 2C, New York, NY 10019

Printed in the United States of America

Library of Congress Catalog Card Number: 82-73811

ISBN: 0-942104-17-X

Distributed by Penguin Putnam, Inc.

40 39 38 37 36 35

To love, which is God . . .
which is Love . . .
which is God . . .
which is Love . . .
which is God . . .

God, with infinite wisdom, gave us the enchantment of sex so that together we may joyfully pleasure each other and create a loving bond that will last a lifetime.

Contents

HOW TO SATISFY
A WOMAN
<u>EVERY</u> <u>TIME</u>...
and have her beg for more!

Author's Note

You cannot have the quadruple whammy of physical, mental, emotional and spiritual ecstasy unless sex is between two people who love each other.

I believe that sex and love belong together in a loving, faithful, committed, married relationship.

This is a marriage manual.

Foreword

I believe in marriage. I also believe in faithfulness in marriage. When one or the other of the partners is unfaithful, the bond of marriage is broken, the trust is shattered. And when that happens, it is difficult if not impossible to keep the marriage alive.

To have a faithful marriage takes two faithful partners. And if *each one* of the partners (not just one) is sexually satisfied, there is no reason to be unfaithful.

I believe God gave us our sex organs to bond us together in pleasure within our marriage. And through this incredible pleasure, to keep us faithful to each other as long as we both shall live.

Almost all women fake orgasms. Women have done this since time began (I give reasons in Chapter 1). Not only are they missing out on one of life's greatest joys, but their husbands and lovers are missing out, too. A woman faking pleasure and a woman pleasured to the depths of her being are two different women. A man's pleasure in sex is magnified tremendously when he has a partner who is giving and receiving the same orgasmic joys, the same explosions of ecstasy, the same expanding of self that carries her to the same far reaches of the universe to which he travels.

A man will be loved as never before when he is able to give his woman the greatest pleasure he can give her—an orgasm. And when he can do this *every time* they make love, her love will know no bounds.

She will never look at another man. She will never need another man. Their union will be bonded as long as they both shall live . . .

Introduction

When I wrote *Isle of View (Say It Out Loud)*, I included in it a short part about sex. After all, the ultimate experience of love is "making love," or sex, between two loving persons. I wrote about THE BIG BANG THEORY, and women faking it. And as I mentioned in the book, I spoke to thousands of women who told me about the problems they had in being satisfied during intercourse by their mates. I interviewed 486 women, not one of whom told me she never faked orgasm. Only 52 told me they occasionally faked it, whereas 124 said they faked it *most* of the time, and 310 said they faked it *every* time. I was astonished, because I thought I was the only one who used to fake it.

I wrote about how a woman can be pleasured so she'll never have to fake it again. I only touched on the subject, I didn't go into real detail. But the response to my TV appearances with the book was overwhelming. I got a letter from a Kansas City newscaster saying that in all his years of broadcasting, he had never had such an incredible response. He said he had hundreds of women and even more *men* calling and writing him asking about that section of my book. And it was the same all over the U.S. TV and radio hosts from Houston, Detroit, Dallas, Minneapolis, Los Angeles, all contacted me with the same phenomenal reactions.

On call-in shows I received hundreds of calls from women, women married eight years, twenty years, thirty-five years, all telling me how they'd been faking it for all the years of their marriages. One woman I'll never forget, who called me on a radio talk show in Miami, told me she'd been married fifty-three years and had never had an orgasm, and had been faking it for all that time. In a darling "little-old-lady-voice" she said very hiply, "You're telling it like it is, Naura!"

A radio host in Cincinnati told me she'd been

married fourteen years and had never had an orgasm. Of course, she didn't tell me this on the air; it was during a commercial break (this isn't something you talk about or admit to in public). I spoke to a PR woman in Detroit who was married over twenty years and who had been faking it for over twenty years.

Every male talk-show host who heard these calls was amazed and truly flabbergasted. They all said they couldn't believe it. And the women talk-show hosts told me privately that having orgasm difficulties certainly was true for them, too. In fact, some of them admitted they'd never had one.

Now the reason it's so easy for women to call in and be so brutally frank is because all the calls are anonymous. On call-in radio shows you don't have to give your name, so these women could be ultra-honest about their sex lives.

Women said they were tired of faking it and putting up with THE BIG BANG THEORY, and men said they were anxious to find out how to *really* pleasure their mates so there wouldn't *be* any more faking orgasms.

Isle of View (Say It Out Loud) did very well,

and I feel I reached a lot of people. But that section on sex was only a few pages, and I felt that after the incredible responses I had gotten, I needed to expand on what I knew, and bring my experience and help to many more people. I needed to write a book on this very important subject.

There's a need for information that is truly staggering, because this need for satisfying a woman has *never* been explained.

There have been hundreds of books written about how to make love to a *man*. And they all tell about fancy and intricate and sensual things you can do to a man's body to arouse him.

Now the thing that seems a little crazy is that it's really quite *easy* to arouse a man. By nature of his anatomy, arousal is not very difficult. I'm talking about a healthy male—not a physically, mentally, or emotionally sick one. A man's sexual organs are all on the outside of his body and are easily stimulated. Seeing a woman pass by—indeed, *thinking* about seeing a woman pass by—is enough to arouse many men. And looking at a nude female can do more than just make him smile and breathe hard.

Certainly boredom with the same dull partner can turn a man off. At that point he might need technique from a woman to turn him back on. But why is his partner dull? Why is she boring? Can it be that *she* is bored? Out-of-her-skull bored? Because the pleasure is all one-sided? I strongly believe that when a man knows how to please a woman, it becomes a double turn-on, and boredom for both of them flies out the window. Sex only gets boring when one of the partners is not enjoying it.

There have been lots of books written about *sex,* and though they go into foreplay and courting and romance and all that, they *all* miss THE MAIN EVENT. A man can be the greatest romancer and foreplay artist and get his woman aroused, and then comes THE MAIN EVENT and he blunders unknowingly, and the woman, also not knowing what he's doing wrong (but absolutely knowing it's *all* wrong!), pretends finally to have an orgasm because she knows that the way he's doing it she'll *never* have one, and she wants to get the whole thing over with to end the boredom and/or pain.

And there have been lots of books written

about how to arouse a woman. They describe foreplay in intimate detail, with all kinds of lotions and props and weird positions and all the things to do to get her ready for an orgasm. But that's only half the story, 'cause as ready as she can get, if the man doesn't know how to handle THE MAIN EVENT—intercourse—she's going to be a *very* frustrated, unhappy, and unsatisfied woman.

And I explain in the first chapter why she will probably fake an orgasm, or else she'll just give up on the relationship. That's when she starts looking around for another man. And can you blame her?

Now I believe *only* a woman can explain the intricacies of satisfying a woman because a man can't *possibly* know this without female input. As I said before, a man, just by nature of his anatomy, is much more easily pleased than a woman. He can't possibly know what the physical sensations are in a woman's body.

And up to now how was a man to learn about how to pleasure a woman? They sure don't teach it in school. They teach how to read and write and add and subtract and spell. You learn the capitals of every state and where Afghanistan is located, but you sure don't learn how to make love. And as I see it, making love is a lot more important than knowing how to conjugate a verb or parse a sentence. So a man gets out of school and starts dating and probably having sex, and it's all hit-or-miss. He just "does what comes natcherly." He gets satisfaction, but the woman doesn't, because he doesn't know what he's doing. He fumbles and grabs and paws, and because it feels good to him, he thinks it also feels good to her. But it doesn't.

And aside from wishing it felt better, how is the woman to know that it should be any different? She also doesn't learn anything in school about making love. She's just as ignorant as he is.

The vast majority of men are definitely inept lovers, but it's not their fault. You can't blame them. How are they to know any better? And if women were any smarter on the subject, they'd teach the men. But they aren't, so the men keep groping and the women keep faking.

Another major reason for the gross ignorance about sex is that almost all romantic novels dealing with scenes of explicit sex are written by men who believe that women love rough, tough, bang-'em-up sex, or by women who, having read these kinds of stories, also think that's what will turn on their readers. After all, it does *sound* sexy.

Why is it that everyone thinks a woman just needs a man to *enter* her to make her roll around wild-eyed in a crazed fashion and scream out in passion? I've read it hundreds of times, and that's the main reason I thought there was something wrong with *me* when I didn't have an orgasm after being "banged." I was brainwashed by writers of sexy fiction, and that's *just* what it is, fiction. *Playboy* and *Penthouse* and all the other men's magazines lead everyone to think that every really sensuous woman needs only to have a man enter her to have her scream with passion and writhe with desire.

Some of the following excerpts are fiction, and some purport to be true. I listed a lot of them because there are so many in every book and magazine around. And as many as I listed, I left out literally thousands more. Some are very well written and some are awful. But they *all* make my point.

"She arched both legs girdling his hips, and impaled herself on him . . . he bore down, her nails knifing his skin, until he pierced her . . . she began to thrust at Fabian, her body springing back as the tip of his flesh met her womb . . . her body sundered, waiting for him to keel into her, offering herself to a deeper quest . . . As she plunged beneath him, her eyes staring, her mouth trapping a scream, he moved into her again, a reeling of ebb and flow pulling her apart, buckling her in quivers of desire . . ."

Passion Play Jerzy Kosinski

"He pushed her legs apart with his hands, and she lay before him, spread-eagled. He mounted her. 'I'm going to plug you, you bitch.' His cock was enormous . . . Then there was only ecstasy . . . as she watched his waxen cock moving in and out . . . 'Don't take it away,' she screamed. 'I love it. Keep fucking me . . . I love it, I love it . . . I love your gigantic, beautiful prick, your hairy cock. I want it to plug me for ever.'"

The Users Joyce Haber

Introduction

"As I entered her ass, she gave a soft moan of pleasure and begged me to go deeper. 'Ram it up me. Please, ram it harder! Harder! Harder!' Soon my thrusts were so forceful that each one nearly knocked her over . . . As we reached orgasm, we were both moaning so loudly that we nearly drowned out the music . . ."

Name and Address Withheld
Penhouse Forum

"She was so hot by the time they had gotten to her cabin that as he untied her bikini the very touch of his hand on her flesh caused her to shudder with orgasm."

The Body Brokers Robert Eaton

"I positioned myself over her and started to thrust gently, but Linda would have none of that. She grabbed me by my ass and pulled me toward her so that my full seven inches were firmly embedded in her cunt. I started to thrust in and out . . . until Linda started to lift her ass off the floor to meet my thrusts. She had to be the best fuck of my life, because she really got into it, not like most of the women I've fucked, who seem to be very passive and require a lot of foreplay."

B.G., Chicago, Illinois
Penthouse Forum

"His lovemaking became frenetic, almost savage, but Karen, later, exhausted and sleepy, told him he was terrific . . ."

Count Me In Fan Nichols

"She lurched her bottom up and locked her legs around his back. He lowered himself into her and she began to writhe and grind her pelvis up against him, muttering strange guttural sounds and grunts of pleasure . . . In a few moments they were thrusting and churning their bodies in a frenzy of excitement . . . then she pushed herself down until she caught up his rigid member again and plunged herself upon it, bouncing up and down, flexing her legs, now squatting, now kneeling. Suddenly she attained a shuddering climax."

Runaway Slave Robert Tralins

"Kevin . . . abruptly flipped me onto my back, entering me with one hard thrust. As he began pumping furiously . . . I wrapped my legs around him and I could feel myself climbing to the heights of ecstasy . . . In two more fierce thrusts he joined me in the climax of a truly beautiful fuck."

L.L., Jacksonville, Florida
Penthouse Forum

". . . He pulled his hand away, and without a pause at all, literally rammed his cock in her cunt so hard it caused his balls to strike her tummy, and a low animal growl of pleasure emanated from her pelvis and erupted . . ."

"Troy," *Men In Love* Nancy Friday

"I barely got the head of my ten-inch member into her when she pleaded with me to stop, but of course I did not. I fucked her ass so hard that I thought she would never walk again, but somehow she handled it and begged me for more."

Name and Address Withheld
Penthouse Forum

"With no warning, no gentle probe, he shoved his prick into Jana and fell on her simultaneously . . . He lifted himself out of her slightly and then fell again more deeply into her . . . grinding his hips into hers . . . pushing in and out, his balls slapping at the skin between her thighs. Jana smiled."

Trading Up Joan Lea

"By this time she was begging for someone to ram a cock in her. I obliged and rammed all eight inches in and gave her a ride."

Name and Address Withheld
Penthouse Forum

"Jack gripped her and drove himself into her. She clutched at him, trying not to scream, and she felt how wildly, helplessly they struggled, how viciously her body grabbed at his in its agony to keep him with her, to force him with her, to force him again and again into her. How she needed him, how raw and crazy was her need for him."

Do With Me What You Will
Joyce Carol Oates

"He fucked like a machine, refusing to succumb to an orgasm himself but urging me to come again and again and again. After the first three times I was sore and wanted to stop. I begged him to stop but he wouldn't. He kept banging away at me like an ax murderer."

Fear of Flying Erica Jong

"Hildy begged me to fuck her. I thrust my huge nine and one-half inch tool into her viselike box. We fucked with a vengeance for what seemed hours. She experienced dozens of orgasms."

T.R.H., Washington, D.C.
Penthouse Forum

"She started bouncing on him, a crazy rhythm, leading him on, and on, bouncing and feinting like the tough, punch crazy fighter she was, till she got him locked in her hug again, poised for her shuddering come."

Doctor Love Gael Greene

"I inserted my swollen member into her love triangle and started to pump her. We climaxed at the same time . . ."

> Name and Address Withheld
> *Penthouse* Forum

"Beau began fucking her hard and then built up momentum. 'No, no, yes, yes,' she muttered. Dear God, this awful pleasure was driving her mad. Joy and pain were intertwined. 'Oh, oh, no, Mr. Kingston, I'm coming—oh—oh.' Miss Holmes' thin body was writhed in ecstasy."

> *March to the Drummer* Peter Dane

Because none of the above quotes is the way it really happens, I'm going to start right out in Chapters 1, 2, and 3 in my book with *explicit instructions* on how a woman can be *really* satisfied. I *guarantee* that if you read them carefully and go about making love as I suggest, you will absolutely, positively be successful in pleasuring your woman *every time.*

And it will be quicker, too. Most men don't have a clue to what they're doing to a woman's body in the sex department, and because of this ineptness, they think it has to take hours to satisfy her. The beauty part of all this is that when a man finds out *exactly* what to do—and does it—it takes just minutes for a woman to have an orgasm once THE MAIN EVENT begins.

And it works. It really does!

How can I guarantee positive results every time? You just read on, put into practice what I've explained, and you'll find out the very first time that it absolutely does work. *Every time!*

1
The Big Bang Theory

Okay, you two are in love, and you're making love. It's fabulous for you—the guy—it's sensual, pleasure-full, and your orgasm is incredible. You love her and you know she also loves you and she says it's great for her, too.

But is it? I'm sure you believe her, and feel that you could tell if she were faking, but you probably don't know that there's *no way* a man can tell if a woman is faking an orgasm. I'm sure you've heard that there *are* ways to tell, like her breathing quickening, her nipples getting hard, etc., but all these things happen when she's aroused, not necessarily when she has an orgasm.

And all you women. You know you can fake it, right? You've been doing it for years. God knows I was. Up till several years ago, I had *never* had an orgasm in the normal way of making love. (The other ways are not abnormal. I use the term normal to mean the usual, or most common way, of malking love, the missionary position. I believe that *this is* the most sexually satisfying to both men and women once the man learns how to really pleasure his mate in this position. Certainly all other ways are pleasure-full, but they gained their great popularity because it is easier for a woman to be satisfied using *some* sort of manipulation of her clitoris, either manually—with fingers—or with lips and a tongue. And women have gotten their men to do these things because they know from experience that's the *only* way they can achieve orgasm. Even though it *is* pleasure-full, it doesn't *begin* to feel as totally and completely satisfying as the normal missionary position, once the man learns how to make love in this wonderful and loving way.)

Again, I had *never* had an orgasm in the normal way of making love. And I faked it. I had faked it all my life. Believe me, I was Bernhardt,

Duse, Bette Davis, and Meryl Streep all rolled up in one. No man ever suspected, *ever,* that I wasn't thoroughly, totally satisfied. And that's because I was such a great actress convincing him. I moaned, I writhed, I gritted my teeth, I did *all* the right things at the right times—and I was completely and utterly unsatisfied and frustrated.

Now some of you men might ask why—why did I go to all that trouble? Why didn't I just tell my guy that I wasn't being satisfied? I didn't for the same reasons that *no* woman wants to tell her guy.

First, she loves her man—really cares for him and that's why they're together in the first place. And she doesn't want to hurt his feelings or his ego. She wants him to feel like a tiger.

Second, she doesn't want him to feel she's not a sensual woman, that maybe there's something wrong with her. She thinks it's her fault, that maybe she's a "frigid" woman. Why else is she unable to have an orgasm when he has such an easy time having one? God forbid the thought should ever cross *his* mind that she's "frigid." That would devastate her. (At this point I'd like to point out that there is *no* such thing as a "frigid" woman. There are only inept male lovers!) And in her mind, if he *did* think she was "frigid," he might go out looking for a hot number to replace her.

And third, she doesn't know *why* she's not having an orgasm. She still thinks it's her fault, but if she only knew *why,* she could do something about it, right? Or she could tell him what to do right if she only knew what he was doing wrong, or that he *was* doing something wrong. He got her excited with foreplay. She's burning up with desire, and as soon as he enters her and starts pumping, she's turned off. That wonderful, excited feeling, that glow all over her body, that tingling in her sex organs, vanishes. Why? Because he's doing his BIG BANG number. In and out, in and out—Bang Bang. He doesn't realize it doesn't feel good to her. It doesn't always hurt at first, but it sure doesn't feel terrific. And after a while of being "banged," it *does* hurt, and she wishes he would get it over with fast!

If you men would just try this experiment, you'd understand exactly what it feels like. Put your left arm out and with your right fist hit your left arm for about thirty seconds (the longer you do it, the more it hurts). I did this on several TV shows to show the male hosts what "banging" feels like, and they were all amazed. They had no idea that that's what happens when a man enters a woman and starts pumping. But if you stop and think about it, it's very logical. A man's penis, ready to make love, is hard. The territory surrounding his penis, his pelvis, is also hard. And a woman's sex organs are all soft. So when a man puts his hard organ into a woman's soft organ and then starts pumping hard, it hits her hard on her clit, and it doesn't feel good. After a few minutes of being hit on her soft organ, it begins to hurt. And just to get it over with, she'll pretend *anything* to stop the pain or boredom. She quickly learns how to pretend she's having an orgasm.

In the next two chapters I'm going to tell you *exactly* what to do to not only arouse your woman, but to take her all the way to the most glorious orgasm she's ever had, and to do this *every time you make love.*

And the beauty part of this is that when she truly has an incredible orgasm that sends off rockets through her whole body, *you* will become more excited than you've ever been before, and your orgasm will surpass any you've ever had before, because now you'll know the real power that you possess to turn her on and send her to the moon, outer space, Mars, Venus, etc. And you'll feel a love from her that you've never felt beforc.

And even if you think you're pretty good now, and your woman tells you that you're a perfect lover, (remember, she loves you and wants you to think you *are* perfect), try it anyway!

And if you've been worried that maybe she's got eyes for someone else, or think maybe she *might* look at another man, after you give her the ultimate pleasure that you're now capable of because *now* you know *how* to pleasure her, you'll realize that there's no *reason* for her to look around or to fool around, 'cause *you're* the man who gives her what she wants and needs and loves.

2
Teasing

Stop and think about what turns you on. A sniff of a wonderful fragrance, a taste of caviar, the touch of velvet on your skin—all soft and gentle things. It's not so pleasure-full to be over-powered by too strong an odor (yech!), or to gorge on a big bowl of zabaglione (double yech!!!), or to be rubbed roughly with any material—velvet included.

Try another experiment. Put your left arm out again and now take the fingers of your right hand and very softly run your fingers over your arm. But very gently. Hardly touch the skin. Make like your fingers are feathers, and tease your skin. It tickles a little, and after a few seconds you feel like you want to scratch it. The soft touch makes a gentle itch that feels good and needs to be satisfied, or scratched.

Well, the same principle applies to making love. First, gently touch her skin—anywhere. A leg, an arm, her back—anywhere. But it *must* be gentle, very soft and teasy. Spend a minute or two there. Then slowly, *very* slowly, work up to her breasts—softly, with the tips and pads of your fingers. But don't touch her nipples—yet!

Create a desire. Make her sweetly suffer with wanting something so badly and not being able to get it when she wants it. Make her sweetly suffer with a desire that you won't give her . . . yet.

When you paw her or roughly maul her (which I call THREEPLAY—'cause it sure ain't foreplay!), that's a turn-off, like too strong an odor. *Deliberately* don't touch her nipples for a few minutes. Deliberately tease her. And after a few minutes of your teasing—above her nipple, below it, and all around it, but *never* right on it, she'll be ready for you to touch it. But *only* softly touch, don't grab or pull or knead.

I'd like to make a *very strong point* here. A woman's nipples are her *most erotic body parts!*

There is a *direct line* from her nipples to her clitoris, and when you gently *tease* her nipples it will drive her *and* her clit absolutely wild with desire for your body. The longer you tease, the sexier she'll feel.

Again, just softly take your fingers and hardly touch her nipples at all. This will begin to drive her crazy. You are teasing her. Keep it up, knowing you're driving her crazy. You are calling the shots, and that alone is a giant turn on. And the soft tease of your fingers makes her want more.

Now put your lips very, very gently on her nipple. Don't suck it or do anything yet. Now gently start to suck (do not pull or bite or tongue it, this must be *super* gentle). The softer you suck, the more she'll be turned on. The easier you do it (even though it might seem too little and too soft to you), the more her clit is going to get excited. (If you don't know her clit, ask her which part of "down there" feels the best when touched—that's her clit, a tiny little miniature penis.)

It shows her *you're* in control, and that's what every woman who loves a man wants her man to be—in charge of her body. The fact that you're holding back and only gently sucking with the soft touch of your lips creates a *divine itch,* an unbelievably strong itch in her clit, and the more it itches, the more she wants you to satisfy that itch.

By holding back, you are creating a tremendous desire within all of her sex organs. After a few minutes of this (and *don't* weaken, and grab or bite or paw), whenever you feel she's ready (and believe me, she'll let you know), if *you're* ready with an aroused and hard penis (if not, I'll cover that a little later—right now we're working on *her), do not put it in her!*

This is the MAIN EVENT coming up, and once you get this right, you'll never have trouble again.

3
The Main Event

Now you are aroused. Your penis is aroused. And she is aroused.

Get in the missionary position—you on top.

DO NOT ENTER HER.

Take your penis in your hand and gently rub her clitoris with it. Gently. *Very* gently. Play with her with your penis very softly. You are letting her know that you *could* go inside her with it, but you're choosing not to. You are going to tease her with it. You are going to build a desire inside her until she begs you to put it in. You are now totally in charge—the master of yourself and of her. You are going to tease her until she literally will beg you to put it in.

You'll be getting to that point soon. You're teasing her clit gently and the more you tease, the more aroused she's getting. Just keep it up, *very* gently teasing her with your penis. She's now asking you to put it in, and you say no, and you keep teasing her with your penis gently rubbing on her clit. Again she asks you to put it in, and again you say no. You continue teasing her and now she says *please* put it in, but you're *still* not ready. You want her to beg, right? Well, give her another minute or so and she will beg. Now remember, you're in charge. It's *your* penis and you can sweetly torture her as long as you want.

And she'll *love* it. She knows you're in charge and in total control of your penis and her body. Before this you were *not* in control. You just shoved it in—Bang Bang—and that was it. No control. No mastery.

All right, now you've finally gotten her to the point of begging you to put it in. So you've decided the time is now. But do you put it in?

NO!

You will *very* gently go in about one-half inch (hardly at all) and then slowly take it out, then slowly back in one-half inch and slowly out again.

She's going to be really going crazy by now—and you're going to love it. And so will she. After all, she never felt like *this* before.

Good grief, does she want you! But you're still in charge and still teasing.

Now you'll put it in one inch and slowly out, and in one inch and slowly out. Now go in a little more, *very* slowly. Maybe one and a half inches. And very slowly out. Don't *ever* go in all the way, till she starts having her orgasm. Just keep teasing her. When you've worked up to *almost* the full length of your penis, slowly withdraw and in again and out again—*very* slowly and very gently.

The reason not to go all the way in with your penis is that when you do, it rams against her clit, and the whole purpose of this is to *tease* her clit—not to hit it, but to create a desire that drives her mad until she has an orgasm.

Now you're still slowly going in and out, *never* all the way, and you can feel her getting more and more aroused. This in turn gets you more and more aroused, because as much as you're teasing her, you're teasing yourself, too. You're totally in command, and both of you know it. And the more you can stall it, the more incredible and intense both your orgasms will be.

Teasing is a form of sweet torture, for both of you. And we all—both men and women—have a touch of masochism within us. The act of surrender, which is the most beautiful part of orgasm, is surrender in love to the one you love.

Okay, you've brought her to the point of surrender—she's begging you to give her the orgasm that her body so desperately wants now, so now you go in just a little deeper, and slowly out, and keep that up until her body begins to quiver, and you will continue going in and out while she has an orgasm that rocks her whole being. She may moan or scream or talk incoherently or just breathe huskily, but this time you'll know she's not faking it. You have *made* her have an orgasm. It wasn't an accident. It didn't just happen. You deliberately and consciously teased her body until she couldn't stand it any longer. She gave herself to you totally and completely because you demanded it. With love, to be sure, but it was a deliberate command for her to respond. She opened up completely to you.

Now if you're in good physical shape, you'll be able to give her several more orgasms after her first one. The ones that follow come much faster and you don't have to tease. Of course, you can't revert to THE BIG BANG, but you can be a *little* more forceful. You'll see how she'll react if you can keep from coming and continue to penetrate her. Usually, within a minute she'll have another and another, as long as you can continue. Usually three to five—some women only two and some over five.

But maybe you're so excited by her first explosion that you just can't hold back, so you have your orgasm. It will be the deepest and fullest orgasm you've ever had, because you've controlled it up to this moment, and you've teased yourself and now you've let yourself go.

Hopefully, you've been able to give her two or three orgasms, but if only one, that's okay, 'cause it was undoubtedly the best one she's ever had, maybe even her first. And next time you can try for more than one.

Now if you want to try something that is sexually incredible, but incredibly difficult to do,

47

get to the point you're at now—the point where you're both seconds away from an orgasm, and stop. Just stop cold. And resume several hours later, or the next morning. Holding back like that will triply excite you when you resume your lovemaking, and you'll both be so sensual and so ready that when you start over again with the teasing, you'll both be tortured with desire, and by the time you gently tease her clit with your penis, she'll be screaming for you to enter her, and when you start gently putting your penis in her a half-inch at a time, she'll be pleading, begging for you to go in more. And when you both have your orgasms, the explosions will rock both of you like you've never been rocked before.

But it takes great control. And a very healthy body (see Chapter 7).

You'll notice how relaxed she is and how loving toward you. After all, you've just given her the greatest experience of her life. And she'll never forget it. Or you.

4
What To Do If Your Man Won't Even Try
(For Women Only!)

If you're a woman and can't get your mate to read this book (he doesn't read books, he doesn't read sex books, he already knows how to make love, he knows some women fake it but *you* sure don't, etc.), *you* read it, and after *you* learn what he's been doing wrong all these years, you'll now be able to gently and sneakily show him what you want, or if you're in love with a *real* hardhead who refuses to change *anything* about the way he makes love, and he's so stubborn he's hanging on to his "great lover" image, all is not lost.

You should *not* continue faking it. In fact, if

you do, you'll be letting your man down, because then he'll *never* learn how inept he is, and he'll *never* change, and *you'll* never have the ecstasy of an orgasm during intercourse. You'll also be letting your *self* down by pretending something that isn't happening.

In Shere Hite's book *The Hite Report,* she lists hundreds of quotes from women who fake it. Here are just a few that might ring a bell:

"I fake orgasms to save his pride and prevent arguments."

"Sometimes it builds a man's ego to let him think he's successful. Therefore, if I really like a man and want him to think I enjoyed sex more than I did, I do it."

"Yes, I always fake orgasms. It just seems polite. Why be rude?"

"I fake them often. He and I have had such an abysmal sex relationship that I don't want to burden him with the knowledge that I don't come during intercourse."

"I *always* did. (I'm sixty-two now.) I was told to

do it by male doctors to keep my husband happy (bless me). I was thinking there was something missing in my makeup for about thirty-five years—and that's a long time to imagine you had to fake it!"

"I have been faking orgasms for thirty years, because I need approval—I lack self esteem—I'm ashamed as though I had a club foot or one eye and because I don't want to hurt my husband, who is also insecure."

"I always fake them during intercourse. I know it would hurt the guy I live with if he knew otherwise, so I always tell him that it was great."

"Yes, it's easier and faster than struggling."

"When he asked if I came, I said yes. Sometimes he would even tell me how many times I came, and I didn't have the heart to tell him that I hadn't come at all."

"I always fake them—because I never have them."

"Like asking if the sky is blue. Yes, during intercourse; I usually don't want men to know I *never* have them."

"For fifteen years I was the world's best faker. Honestly—I think they should have a phallic trophy—mounted on a pedestal (like in the art history books) for *all women*—I think they all fake it with men."

As I mentioned earlier in the book, up till a few years ago, I had never had an orgasm during intercourse and *I always* faked it. And I honestly thought I was the only woman doing this. Of course, I never ever told a single soul, man or woman, that I was not able to orgasm in intercourse. I was embarrassed and I didn't want *anyone* to know that I was not "normal"—HA! This was a little before everyone talked so freely about sex, and before all the very explicit books were written about women's sexual problems. So from all I read in popular fiction and from all I heard, I certainly thought all other women had an easy time climaxing during intercourse. All my friends and acquaintances must have been as anxiety-ridden as I was about this lack in their lives, and they sure weren't going to tell me or anyone else about their "frigidity problem." They obviously were as upset and embarrassed as I was, and they were all faking it exactly the same as I was.

The difference now is that because women are admitting their problems, probably very few think they are the only ones faking it. Hopefully, even fewer think they're "frigid."

Here are some more quotes from *The Hite Report* about how so many women think they are, or thought they were, "frigid":

> "I went along for thirty-four years carrying the burden of not having vaginal orgasms, never telling anyone because I felt something was wrong with me—I thought I was frigid."

> ". . . It's going to take some time, and I believe eventually a woman will have to tell me how to have an orgasm during sex. Right now I don't know who to ask plus I will have to be quite careful in discussing this—because I wouldn't want someone to think I was abnormal."

> "I fake them to avoid confrontation with a man, to avoid explaining why I was like I was, to avoid their trite responses of lesbianism, frigidity, etc."

"Yes, for ten and a half years! I didn't want anyone to think I was frigid."

". . . if I don't have any—then it's my fault, and my boyfriend doesn't want to have intercourse very much if I am frigid."

In *The Redbook Report on Female Sexuality,* a woman is quoted about her unhappy and unsatisfied sex life, and what her doctor told her about it:

". . . After 10 years of never having an orgasm, I finally got up the courage to ask my family doctor (they always tell you to ask the family doctor, right?), as my marriage was falling apart. His response was, 'Seventy percent of all women are frigid—it's all in your head.'"

Just as I thought it was only *my* problem (never dreaming it could *possibly* be my man's ineptness), these women all think they are, or thought they were, "frigid."

Again, please remember, *there is no such thing as a frigid woman.* Once men really learn how to intercourse, *every woman will respond!*

Now lots of women think they have to masturbate during intercourse to achieve orgasm, but this is *not* true. When you get your man to make love exactly as in Chapter 3, you do not have to do *anything* to your self—he does it all. Here are just a few quotes from *The Hite Report* about women who orgasm during intercourse, but *only* with masturbation.

> "I would like to have orgasm during inter-course *without* having to play with my clitoris at the same time! If I didn't do that I would almost never come."

> ". . . I have orgasms from masturbation and cli-toral stimulation *only.* I feel very little, and rarely, from penis penetration, and I've *never* had an orgasm from penis stimulation . . ."

> "I would like to have orgasm during intercourse *without* having to play with my clitoris at the same time. If I didn't do that I would almost never have orgasms. I would like to be able to have them with just intercourse . . ."

In *The Redbook Report on Female Sexuality* the authors state:

"Should intercourse be taken literally—orgasms that occur during penetration—or generally—orgasms that occur during a sexual episode, including manual or oral stimulation? The distinction is not trivial for the millions of women who are easily orgasmic by mouth, hand, and vibrator but for whom the penis is just a pleasant accompaniment to the blissful harmonies."

"I have conducted my own little survey and I do not have one friend or acquaintance who has ever had a "real" orgasm through intercourse—only through clitoral stimulation . . ."

"I have never had an orgasm during sexual intercourse. To have an orgasm, I must have cunnilingus or manual clitoral stimulation. I know of women today who are faking orgasm during intercourse because they are too embarrassed to tell their husbands or lovers that no matter how long they keep their erection, they just can't make her have an orgasm. *Please, please* discuss this when you print the results of your survey! . . ."

Dr. Seymour Fisher, who wrote *The Female Orgasm,* did a study of over three hundred women, and of these women, 80 percent said they needed masturbation during intercourse in order to have an orgasm.

Alfred Kinsey of the "Kinsey Report" *(Sexual Behavior in the Human Female)* reported that "the techniques of masturbation and of petting are more specifically calculated to effect orgasm than the techniques of coitus itself." Kinsey says that for most women, intercourse alone always or almost always results in *no* orgasm, and that intercourse with masturbation for these same women almost always results in orgasm.

Dr. Debora Phillips, who wrote *Sexual Confidence,* says:

". . . a woman is less likely to have an orgasm during intercourse than through manual or oral stimulation. (For those who would rush into intercourse as the *goal* of lovemaking, it's interesting to note that many women actually experience a *decline* in sexual pleasure with penetration.)"

Dr. Helen Singer Kaplan, Dr. David Reuben, and Masters and Johnson, have all written about masturbation as a means of attaining orgasm during intercourse for most women who cannot climax without it.

So—your mate is a lousy lover who won't admit it or change, you found out you *don't* have to masturbate during intercourse, and you're *not* going to fake it anymore. What *are* you going to do?

You are now going to take charge of the situation, and by doing this, control your love life and be sexually satisfied every time you make love.

Of course, solving your own problem by yourself is *not* as sensational as having a loving partner who tries to change and become a better lover because he accepts and admits the fact that he's inept. Listen, almost every man is, so it's nothing to be ashamed about. He never wanted to be, and till now he didn't really realize that he was inept. But hopefully he's read this book and is willing to try to make you happy.

But your problem now is that you are in love with a *real BIG BANG* artist, and he can't (or won't) accept the fact that he's a terrible lover. And you're so much in love with him that you want to stick with him, awful lover or not. So what do you do?

Well, first of all, you *don't* tell him he's inept. In fact, no woman should *ever* tell her man that he's been a bad lover. Even if you've been faking it for thirty-five years, don't ever tell him that. Why hurt him now? After all, he wasn't inept deliberately, and you didn't know what to tell him to do either, right? The point is you can't do anything about the past—it's all over with and you can't recapture all those missed ecstasies—so let's start with *NOW.* Again, hopefully he's read this book and is now a fantastic lover (it's so *easy* to be one once you know what to do and what not to do).

If your husband is not a take-charge kind of guy, you can give yourself an orgasm using his penis. Start by turning him on and gently sucking his penis and watching it grow bigger and bigger, till it's now all nice and wet. Then lie down next to him and let him turn you on by super gently teasing your nipples with his lips and driving you crazy with desire (and you must let him know that the softer his lips are, the bigger the turn-on). Now get in the missionary position (he's on top). Take his erect penis and gently rub your clit. Have him continue to softly *(very* softly) suck your nipples as you keep rubbing your clit with his erect wet cock (this will feel *very* sexy to him as you get more and more aroused). You won't believe *how* sexy playing with yourself with his penis will feel, and how close to an orgasm you will feel from the very beginning. Keep it up till you have a clit orgasm (close to heaven); then as you're orgasming, put his penis inside you and as he starts to move in and out (you'll find your own rhythm and so will he), you will have another orgasm. But this second one will be a vaginal orgasm and stronger than the first, and this *is* heaven! You may even have more than one and they will keep getting stronger. It's an incredible experience, not as great as if *he* plays with your clit with his penis, but a close second. Both of you will have the best orgasm you've ever had, and something to look forward to is that it gets even better when *he* decides to take charge of your body.

And now here's even *another* way a woman can control her sexual destiny and have a climax every time with a man who hasn't picked up on, or refuses to learn, teasing.

This time you do it with your thighs. When a man comes on too strong and too hard and starts banging, just squeeze your thighs, which will clamp around his hips and keep his body from ramming your body, and slow him down. Slowly, as he finds out he can't "bang" you because you won't *allow* it, he'll start to ease up his attack because he really can't do anything else.

Now when I say squeeze your thighs, I mean *take control.* You have some very strong thigh muscles there that are hardly ever used, and the more you use them, the stronger they get. When you squeeze your thighs, you also control how much of his penis you allow inside you. Not only will he not be able to ram you, he will only be able to go in as much and as far as you want. So you can tease yourself with his penis and do all the things that in Chapter 3 *he* will do to you, only now *you're* in charge. It's not as super duper as when *he* does it all, but you definitely can have an orgasm this way, and he will undoubtedly eventually become aware of what you want and what pleasures you.

Once you have shown a man that you know what you want, and he starts to pick up on it, and he knows that you know what you want, and he begins, gently and lovingly, to move in and out, you can begin to relax and let him take over more. And every time you make love and show him what you want and how you want it, he will subconsciously begin to remember, so that each time he'll bang a little less hard and you won't have to flex those thigh muscles as hard. Eventually (hopefully after only the first time, but maybe it'll take two or more times), he will totally understand how you *don't* want him to bang you, and how you *do* want him to make love to you in a really teasy and loving way. When a woman is physically relaxed, she will be mentally and emotionally relaxed, too. If he gets too rough again, just flex those thigh muscles to signal him to gentle it (not that maybe later you won't want it a little stronger, but you *start* with it teasy). Then, as he gently and lovingly and teasingly makes love, you can relax and begin to surrender yourself to him, slowly, as he will to you. Sexual surrender is the ultimate in trust—and the ultimate in pleasure. When you're totally open physically, trusting mentally, and vulnerable emotionally is when the rockets explode.

And exploding rockets with the one you love is what life is all about!

5
Lovingness

I'm a total romantic. I believe in everything romantic. I believe love is the most important thing in the world. I know it is for me.

Whenever I talk about sex, I mean sex with love. Without love, sex is an exercise—a pleasant one, to be sure—but still just an exercise.

Aah, but sex with love . . . that's the greatest experience in the world—bar none! I can't think of one thing that feels better physically, mentally, or emotionally.

Now the ability to love is something we all have, but not all of us use it. There are lots of reasons for this. We're afraid, we're tense, we're angry, we're anxious, we're depressed. Unfortunately, all of these negatives keep us from being loving. So it's up to all of us to try as hard as we can to get rid of all the negs in our lives. In Chapter 7 I cover the physical part of health, and I believe when the body is *truly* healthy, then the mind and emotions will be healthy, too.

So in this chapter I don't want to talk about feeling *loving*, but feeling *loved*. Receptive to love. Opening yourself to love. Not feeling guilty or unworthy of love.

Here is my emotional exercise that I do *every* day of my life to help me feel loved.

Every morning, at the end of my twenty sit-ups on my slant-board, I just lie there and close my eyes and totally relax (if you don't have a slant-board, you can lie flat on your bed, without a pillow.) Then I remember emotionally what it was like when someone *really* loved me (mother, father, husband, wife—it makes no difference who, but you must remember the *feeling* of being loved, the wonderful physical glow, and warmth, and open feeling, of someone truly loving you). This takes real concentration and you must be relaxed, but it's really fun. Just be still and go back in time and remember incidents of being held by your mother, or hugged by your dad, or praised by either one of them. You might remember lying on a beach as a kid, under a warm sky, and seeing your mother or dad, and feeling secure and warm and loved with them sitting nearby. It doesn't matter *how* you recapture the feeling of being loved, as long as *something* in your past warms you and opens you up emotionally in its memory.

While doing this, it's very important to smile broadly, because that'll help you to feel loved and happy. Again, you don't force a smile when you feel truly loved, you can't *help* but smile! So when you're relaxed and smiling, you'll know the right feeling is there.

My biggest problem was that I never felt I deserved anything. I felt only guilt for wanting good things for myself. Maybe it was my super-religious upbringing with hell and guilt, etc., or maybe it came from somewhere else, but there it was, coloring everything I did. No wonder I repelled myself from getting good things from my life—I didn't feel I deserved them. But doing this emotional exercise *every day,* and without exception, makes me know I'm loved, and makes me *feel* like I'm a lovable person who deserves everything I desire.

And every single day I feel more and more loved, and more and more lovable, and this *automatically* makes me a more loving person.

Feeling loved makes you realize the *goodness* within yourself, and that goodness is your REAL SELF, or my GIANT SELF, as I call the goodness within me.

Feeling loved makes you feel your oneness with the universe.

And feeling loved in your marriage makes you feel your oneness with your spouse.

Now, a very important part of marriage that many men are not aware of (and not many women are either) is that if a woman doesn't *respect* her husband, doesn't look up to him as a strong person (weak is what she *doesn't* want) who warrants respect, she won't have an orgasm through *his* efforts.

This is very important to know and understand, because if she feels all respect for him is gone, if she feels he's not capable of taking charge of her body (not her life, not her money, but her *body!*) sexually, she will either look around for a man who turns her on (and to be "turned on" a woman must have respect for that man), or she will close up physically and emotionally and be grateful she doesn't have to have sex anymore. She's at the point where she doesn't *want* an orgasm, but the truth is she won't *allow* herself to have an orgasm because an orgasm is *sexual surrender,* and she doesn't *want* to surrender to this weak man for whom she has little or no respect.

Inner strength is *very* sexy.

How do you command respect from a woman who no longer feels that you're worthy of it, who feels you're too weak to *take charge* of anything? You obviously can't force it, but you *can* slowly coax it from her.

Respect can start in the bedroom. If you don't make much money, you're not a titan of industry, you drive a beat-up old car, never mind. All you need is the *attitude* of take charge, the letting her know that you *sexually* are stronger than she is.

If you learn how to drive her crazy in bed and *make* her have an orgasm every time you have intercourse, you will have love like you've never had before. Trust me, she will respect the fact that you are no longer tentative, that you are now in charge of her body (and as you hopefully already know, she's in charge of your body).

A totally sexually satisfied woman will do *anything* for her man, and you'll soon find out how *much* she'll do once you've given her this total pleasure.

Why would she lose the respect for you in the first place? She probably romantically fantasized when you met and got married that you were a strong person who would take care of her in all areas. Remember, inner strength is sexy. Even if she was more successful than you at that time, she still wanted a man who would be able to take care of her if necessary *(all* women in love, subconsciously or consciously, want this).

Maybe you're basically a more passive type of person than she, and maybe you've had business reverses and you both fight now about finances—whatever it is, the respect she had for you (and whatever inner strength she thought you had) at the beginning is gone. It's now up to you, her husband, to learn how to play the game of sex.

> Love should *never* be a game . . .
> Sex should *always* be a game . . .

The games people play in *LOVE* can be very destructive—she flirts with another guy and her husband gets jealous. He makes goo-goo eyes with the hostess at the party and his woman gets crazy with insecurity.

Games like that are not fun, *ever.*

Love should bring security and warmth and a feeling of togetherness and the fun of compatibility, not the fear and jealousy that come from flirting games.

Sex, on the other hand, should be fun from the start. Two people who love each other can drive each other wild with desire by playing the "teasing game" because it's so important to great sex.

I keep coming back to teasing. I was the very first one who came out with it in 1982 with this marriage manual, because it's the bottom-line answer to the greatest physical pleasure you can have.

Start getting your mate excited, and then stop for a minute. Restart and get her even more excited, and stop again.

Now there isn't a doubt who's in charge, is there? And if your mate complains and says she doesn't like that, believe me, its because the recipient of teasing has *totally* lost control. But basically this is what the giant turn-on in sex is all about: SEXUAL SURRENDER.

And one of the most important things I've learned since this book first came out is that even though most women are ready, willing, and able to respond to the man they love, to surrender sexually to him, there are some women who won't allow an orgasm to happen. I started to become aware of this from quite a few husbands who wrote me or told me that their wives either won't let them try the technique, or if they get as far as actually trying it, the women make them stop.

At first this puzzled me, but then in 1991 I received the fourteen-page handwritten letter I mentioned earlier (at the back of the book, on page 137) from a married man who tells about his wife of eighteen years who'd had practically no sexual pleasure in all those eighteen years. He was sure she was frigid, but after he tried the technique, he found out how "hot" she really was. But he had to *make* her have an orgasm. She fought him all the way and actually got angry, but he didn't allow her to make him stop, he just continued with the technique (he says he sensed he was finally on the right track) as she got angrier and angrier, till she finally erupted with sexual ecstasy beyond anything he'd ever imagined could happen. He says it changed his marriage and it changed his life.

It really got me thinking as I reread the letter over and over again. An orgasm is sexual surrender, and women who control their husbands are afraid of giving up that control, and are therefore unable and unwilling to surrender sexually.

Now, many women are *so* afraid of losing control that they keep their husbands as little boys. But this makes the wives unable to have an orgasm, because again, an orgasm is sexual surrender, and you don't surrender to a child, you surrender to someone you look up to and admire, and love. And of course, some men *like* to be treated as little boys because this relieves them of any husbandly responsibilities.

And very importantly, if you, her husband, are not a sweet and loving person who lets her know and feel that you really love her, that's another reason for her to be afraid to surrender sexually.

(Note to wives: Once you read *HOW TO SATISFY A MAN EVERY TIME . . . and have him beg for more!* and start *focusing*—really focusing—on his penis, the love tide will turn!) It's much easier for a woman to surrender to her husband when she feels loved and cherished.

The need for control is based on fear, the fear that if they give up the control, they will lose their husbands, but the way to hold a man is through exciting sex (I didn't say love and I didn't say sex, I said *exciting* sex), and never through control. All a man has to do to get around his wife's control is to lie to her and sneak around to do whatever he wants. Through *exciting* sex he's there because he *wants* to be.

And where could that fear that so many women have come from? Maybe their mommies or poppies scared them about a lot of things, including sex (fear usually doesn't come in single packages), or maybe they had terrible relationships with previous males who treated them badly emotionally and/or left them. There are lots of reasons why people are afraid to trust, but unless you trust, you can't surrender. This is why one-night stands are so fruitless and in fact so destructive. You can't surrender to a stranger who not only is not in love with you, he/she may hurt you, might be a violent person physically or a cruel person emotionally. Either way, it causes pain and further lack of trust.

Also, if a woman is angry at her spouse (either a low-grade constant or a flare-up intermittent), she'll tense up and you could try for an hour and she won't respond (she won't surrender). But when you either make up or find out the reason for the underlying anger and actively work on replacing it with respect, trust, and love, that love will start flowing again and so will her juices.

And if your wife is "cold" and unresponsive, logic tells you that sex is obviously not pleasurefull to her, because if it were, she'd be as "hot" as you are. So it's up to you to learn how to drive her crazy with desire.

Now a very important part of feeling loved is feeling your man will not cheat on you, feeling he loves you as much as you love him, that he will always be faithful (". . . *and keep him faithful forever!*" is the subtitle of *HOW TO SATISFY A MAN EVERY TIME . . .*).

Cheating on your wife is in reality only cheating

on yourself. A clandestine affair might seem exciting (in your mind or in actuality when it happens), but it *cannot* compare with giving an orgasm to the woman you married, the woman whom you love and with whom you share everything in your life. And when you *do* learn how to give her this incredible God-given pleasure, you might be amazed at how *she* will become a more exciting person to be around, and how that life-numbing boredom that led you to think about possibly cheating (or maybe actually doing it) will disappear once excitement with an excited spouse has entered your life.

And of course, the *only* reason a woman would cheat on the man she loves and is married to and wants to spend the rest of her life with is because she's sexually frustrated, she keeps "getting to the edge of the cliff" and never goes over it. This is about the most horrendous physical frustration that any human body can endure. Men can't even *imagine* getting to the point of *almost* having an orgasm and never having it because they never experience that. It's truly beyond their comprehension. And some women have endured this for years!

Many women have told me that sex is not that important, that they're really looking only for affection, only for hugs and "I love you's," but trust me, if her husband takes the time and trouble to learn how to give her an orgasm every time they intercourse, *that's* the kind of affection that will keep her faithful and will let her know you cared enough to learn how to *show* her she's loved. And who says the hugs and "I love you's" won't be there with the orgasm? Why do so many women think it's either one or the other, not both?

The bottom line is that every woman who loves a man wants to surrender to that man, wants him to *make* her have an orgasm through intercourse, but up till now he didn't know how. But once he learns how and lovingly teases her and drives her wild and then makes her come in this extraordinary way, this will create incredible respect (he took control of my body) and love (he cares enough to make this unbounded ecstasy happen for me), and intimacy (I feel closer than I ever thought possible to the man I love).

So it takes the love of the husband to understand the possible problem and to have the strength to *take charge* in the sexual arena. The problem only happens if the man *believes* it when his wife tells him "It doesn't feel good," "Stop," "Don't do that anymore," etc. When he's making love with the technique, some women are *subconsciously* afraid of losing control, even though that's what they really want. And that fear can only be overcome when it's replaced by love. A woman must know her husband loves her, and he must *take charge* of her body. He cannot be intimidated by her. He must realize that every woman deep down desires her man to take control of her body—not her life, not her money, but her body—and he *must take charge* of her body.

This is why love and faithfulness and commitment and marriage are so important to a truly happy sex life. When you're in love and are loved in return by someone you want to spend the rest of your life with, someone you trust totally, you will allow him to take charge of your body and give you sexual nirvana every single time you make love.

You cannot have a great marriage without that deep sexual intimacy. This is what being "in love" is all about, and this is why I wrote this book. . . .

6
Sexual Power

Not only is it tremendously exciting for a man to feel sexual power over the woman he loves, it is even *more* exciting for his wife to feel his sexual power. But some women are afraid of a man's sexual power.

I can't tell you how many times women have called me on live call-in talk-radio shows and screamed at me that every married woman should be in control of her own orgasm and should learn to masturbate so she's not dependent on her husband.

I have argued that the only reason women say this (and write books about it) is because these women have given up on their husbands *ever* learning how to give them orgasms through intercourse, and how sad this is.

But once a husband learns how to do this, real sexual excitement will take over the marriage, and if he felt love from her before, he won't *believe* the love he's going to feel from her now.

As I mentioned before, after I did the survey of 486 married women from all over the country in 1980, I found out that I was not the only woman "faking" it with my husband (remember, this was 1980 and nobody talked about faking then; it was still in the closet). Up till then I honestly thought I was the only one, and I also thought there was something wrong with me, because every time we made love, my *husband* had an orgasm, so there was obviously nothing wrong with *him*—it had to be me.

This ultimately led to my divorce. Let me give you a short scenario on why marriages break up and why husbands and wives cheat. Everyone is looking for a "soul mate." I don't care who you are, a bachelor-type man or a career-oriented woman; underneath it all there is a longing to find your "better half" and become a perfectly together whole.

Now two people meet, fall in love, and get married, each confident that the other is the missing half, the long-sought-after soul mate.

The first few months are divine, and then once in a while the wife will get a little testy and he responds testily. If an orgasm gives endorphins, her body is screaming out for the missing endorphins resulting from the missing orgasms. And as more months go by, more spats.

How many men could go six months or a year without an orgasm or hardly ever having one? And how cranky, crabby, bitchy would *he* be if he *did* go six months or a year without one?

So she bitches about the top he left off the toothpaste tube, the bills, etc., and he screams back. But she's not bitching about bills or toothpaste tops; her body is very tense and nervous, making her mind and spirit tense and nervous just as his would be if *he* never got satisfaction.

As the spats continue and slowly worsen after several years, and the yelling gets louder, each starts to think, "This can't possibly be my soul mate. I made a mistake." And each starts to secretly re-look for a new and different soul mate. And the marriage is figuratively over.

And again, when they go before the judge for the literal ending of the marriage, they both will cite financial problems as the cause, because most people do.

But if the love they once shared had been nurtured by sexual satisfaction for *both* of them, not just the husband (and this *always* strengthens the bond of love), no financial problems, no problems of *any* kind, could have split them up.

Sex is much more important than many people give it credit for. Love is the *most* important part of any relationship, especially marriage, but sex is the deepest *expression* of that love. And if the love is not being expressed sexually for either partner, the marriage is doomed, either to an eventual divorce or a life full of bitching and fighting, and devoid of joy.

When a husband and wife love each other, sexual pleasure *is* the cement that holds that marriage together.

My experience with my then-husband was very similar to what I just described. I didn't say to myself, "I'm not having orgasms, I want a divorce." What happened was I became cranky, crabby, bitchy, and yelled at my husband, who of course yelled back, and the fights escalated.

Again, so many times in divorce court the husband and wife will tell the judge they fought over money. But the truth is if the love and sex are still there, a tow truck could be repossessing their car in full view of the couple (they obviously have money problems, right?), and the wife will *not* yell at her husband; she will feel loved and part of the marital "team," and will work *with* him to solve their problems.

Back to 1980, in that survey *every* woman said that she faked it at least *some* of the time, and the great majority said they faked it every time, just as I did.

After my survey, having found out there was nothing wrong with me, that faking is a universal problem, I came up with my foolproof technique for intercourse (done a *little* bit different than usual).

In 1994 I did a *second* survey of married women, this time 1,102 of them. Here's a copy of that survey:

SURVEY OF MARRIED WOMEN

1. How long have you been married? _____
2. How old are you? _____
   Month, Day, Year _____
3. Are you a religious person? _____ What religion? _____
4. How many times have you been married? _____
5. Have you ever been unfaithful in this marriage? _____
6. Have you ever been unfaithful in another marriage? _____
7. Have you ever thought about being unfaithful? _____
8. Do you have children? _____ How many boys? _____
   How many girls? _____
9. Does your husband ever use oral sex with you? _____
   Did he offer to do this the first time, or did you ask him to? _____
10. Do you have an orgasm every time through oral sex? _____
11. Does your husband ever use his hands to bring you to orgasm? _____
12. Have you *ever* had an orgasm through intercourse *alone,* (husband on top)? _____
    If so, what percentage of the time does this happen? _____
13. Have you ever masturbated? _____
    When you have, do you always have an orgasm: _____
    Most of the time? _____ Sometimes? _____ Never? _____
14. Do you ever masturbate during intercourse? _____
15. Do you ever masturbate during any lovemaking with your husband? _____
16. Have you ever had an orgasm? _____
17. Is having an orgasm important to you? _____
18. If during lovemaking you don't have an orgasm, are you angry? _____
    Do you resent it? _____
19. Were you in love with your husband when you got married? _____
20. Are you in love with your husband now? _____
21. Do you *like* your husband? _____
22. Do you feel an emotional intimacy with your husband? _____

SURVEY OF MARRIED WOMEN

23. Do you use oral sex on your husband? _____ Do you enjoy it? _____

24. During intercourse, would you prefer to be on top? _____

25. Would you like to have intercourse every day if you knew you would have an orgasm in less than 10 minutes? _____

26. Do you feel that affection (hugs, kisses, etc.) is *more* important than having an orgasm? _____

27. Do you feel that men are selfish and are only interested in their own satisfaction? _____

28. Do you feel your husband is sexually selfish? _____

29. How old were you when you first made love? _____

30. How old were you when you first had an orgasm? _____

31. Do you feel your husband is concerned that you are possibly not sexually satisfied? _____

32. Have you ever faked an orgasm with your husband? _____

33. Have you ever faked an orgasm with any man? _____

34. If you do fake or have ever faked an orgasm with your husband, why do you or did you do it? _____
    1) I wanted to make my husband feel he is a good lover. _____
    2) I think there might be something wrong with me and I don't want him to think maybe I'm frigid. _____
    3) It takes so long, I want to get it over with. _____
    4) Other _____

35. Do you think that some women may be naturally "frigid"? _____

36. Would you ever tell your husband you've been faking it or have ever faked it? _____

37. Are you afraid to tell your husband you're faking it or have ever faked it? _____

38. Do you smoke? _____ How much? _____ Do you drink? _____ How much? _____

39. Have you ever told or shown your husband what to do to you to make sex better for you? _____

SURVEY OF MARRIED WOMEN

40. Are you affectionate? Very _____ moderately _____
    hardly _____ not at all _____

41. Is your husband affectionate? Very _____ moderately _____
    hardly _____ not at all _____

42. Do you think a woman can be happily married without ever (or
    hardly ever) having an orgasm? _____

43. Do you think you can have a deep emotional intimacy with your
    husband without you, the wife, having an orgasm when you make
    love? _____

44. Do you think it's just as important for a woman to have an orgasm
    as it is for her husband? _____

45. Would you like your husband to take sexual control of your
    body? _____

46. Would you like to take sexual control of your husband's
    body? _____

47. Would you like taking turns being in sexual control of each other's
    body? _____

48. Do you consider yourself happily married? _____

49. Do you think your husband is happily married? _____

In this survey, fourteen years after my first one,
not all of the women said they faked it; this time
many said they don't even bother to fake it, they
just lie there while he has an orgasm, and then
they get their husbands to use oral sex or hands
to give them one (or the husband gives oral sex or
hands to her first; *then* he has his orgasm in intercourse), which of course won't have to be done
once he learns *how* to intercourse.

By the way, a husband should *not* ask his wife
if she fakes it—of *course* she's going to say no.

She fakes it because she doesn't want him to know she's not having an orgasm, and *that's* because she loves him, is sensitive to his feelings, instinctively knows how important being a good lover is to him *(all* we women instinctively know that), and also doesn't want him to think she's "frigid" (and of course there's no such thing as a frigid woman, only a woman whose husband hasn't learned how to make her "hot!").

There's enormous ignorance, and it's not just the husband's ignorance. If the wife knew what to tell him to do, she'd tell him. I was just as ignorant as my husband all those years I was faking it.

So ignorance is to blame for sexual unfulfillment, not lack of love.

But several of my questions in the second survey, and the answers, I think, you'll find *very* interesting.

I asked, "Would you rather be in control sexually or have your husband in charge?" and 88 percent said husband in charge. Many of the 12 percent who would rather be in control themselves had never had, or hardly ever had, an orgasm. In fact, 11 percent of the 1,102 women surveyed had never had an orgasm.

And 46 percent of the women thought all men

are selfish, but 79 percent thought only their *husbands* were selfish (interesting, no?), which would lead many wives to think of cheating, thinking, "Maybe there's a guy out there who won't be selfish like my husband and who will care enough to give me an orgasm because my husband sure doesn't care" (not realizing, of course, it's ignorance, *not* lack of caring).

And 56 percent of the married women replied that they believe some women are frigid. I find this sad because so-called frigidity is only the ignorance of both spouses.

Both my surveys were enlightening and I believe accurate because they were 100 percent anonymous. Many surveys are one-on-one, and I believe most people will not be totally frank when talking to a person, but *will* be when alone, filling out a form anonymously.

And the one thing I absolutely am positive about is that men are *not* selfish (even though many women in the survey said "all men are selfish").

Any man who loves a woman enough to marry her, to want to spend the rest of his life with her, would do *anything* to give her an orgasm; he just doesn't know how. But once he learns my technique and his wife starts having an orgasm every time they make love, both of them will be amazed at how their love will grow and how much better their marriage is going to be.

Now, fantasies are a part of sexual power and are wonderful. They take ordinary experiences and transform them into imaginative flights to the unknown. They can be exciting, sexy, erotic, stimulating, fun, relaxing—all kinds of different things.

We all fantasize about a new car, a gorgeous mansion, a yacht of our own to take us to our own private tropical island where we'll never have to work again. Just get up, pick breakfast, swim in the lagoon, laze in the sun, make love, and sleep a peaceful sleep under the stars.

Where our fantasies start differing in sex is how we see ourselves. Some men fantasize about power in love, and some women fantasize about helplessness in love. However, I've known men who fantasize about helplessness and are very passive in sex, and I've known women who fantasize about power and are very active in sex. And I'm not talking about very weak men and very strong women. Some of the strongest, most successful men in business, real titans of industry, want to be treated as pussycats and fantasize all kinds of masochistic delights (to them), and some of the weakest-appearing, most docile types of women are tigers and fantasize about power. So you can't tell from looks or appearances.

A fantasy is just that—imaginative. It can't hurt you or anyone else because it's all in your mind.

Now I don't think fantasizing someone else in place of the person you're with is constructive. That's negative, not positive. After all, if you'd rather be with someone else, you shouldn't be with the person you're with.

And of course I believe totally in faithfulness, so that precludes fantasizing group sex.

Really constructive fantasizing is taking the person you're actually with and imagining a situation with him or her that turns you on—really stimulates you mentally, emotionally, and sexually.

How can that be bad? You're using your power of imagination (mind's dominant power) and using it to put excitement into a *real* situation. And if you feel like telling your partner what turns you on, go ahead and do it. If not, don't.

Some women fantasize being spanked. If you've always wanted to fantasize this and it seems your partner is just not the type, well, use your vivid imagination *(all* imaginations are vivid, and like a muscle, they get stronger with use, so the more you use your imagination, the more vivid it becomes). Fantasize your man as the type who *would* want to spank you. And realize that every person, man or woman, reacts differently in different situations. Who may appear as a Caspar Milquetoast or Wilbur Wimp may have all kinds of strong and kinky desires lurking beneath the surface. Just use your imagination and realize that it *is* possible—he *could* be harboring a secret desire to spank you. You don't have to tell him what you want (unless you decide you'd like to). You can just keep fantasizing all you want, and he'll never know what's going on inside your mind.

And then again, you may not know what's going on in *his* brain either. He may have an incredible imagination and may be fantasizing you doing all kinds of wonderful things to him.

For instance, lots of men love to imagine that their woman is stronger than they are, and capable of ordering the man to do the woman's bidding— *whatever* it is. Some *men* like to fantasize being spanked by their wives. It really turns them on.

I know a woman who gets turned on by tickling. She imagines she's being tickled by her husband, and this feeling of losing control really excites her. Her husband hadn't a clue to what was going on in her mind, but she eventually told him, and he loves being *The Tickler* and turning her on so gigantically.

I could list a lot of different fantasies, but the whole point is to make up your own. *You* know you have strong feelings and desires—and you *also* have a strong imagination.

USE IT!

Again, like a muscle, it gets stronger with use. And your own personal fantasies will get even more fantastic!

The beauty part of fantasies is that you can interchange them. One day you can be a powerful person, commanding and vigorous—a real martinet—and the next day you can be a weak person, reveling in your own weakness—helpless, defenseless, and *very* sexy in your helplessness. Or if power *really* turns you on, or weakness does, use one or the other *all* the time.

It's easy, it's fun, it hurts no one, and it just might add spice to your already terrific sex life.

Just remember—in fantasies, *anything* goes ! ! !

7
A Healthy Body

We may fall in love mentally or emotionally or spiritually—mentally you observe someone and you think you like what you see—a great smile, sensational legs, gorgeous eyes, an incredible body. Your thought processes race along, and you decide to further pursue this person. Then your emotions begin to function—feelings begin to play within you—a great sense of humor, quick bright mind, ethics, honesty—which start urging you to get to really know this person. And spiritually you feel that this may be the missing half of yourself for which you've been so eagerly searching for such a long time.

But all these thoughts and feelings and longings can't happen without a body, and cannot be fulfilled without a body. Without your body you can't think, you can't feel, and you can't desire. Your body is the vessel, the instrument, through which all of these things are expressed. Your body is truly the temple of God, although God knows most of us don't treat it so religiously. Most of us brutally mistreat ourselves until it's a wonder we can function at all. No wonder we have a problem thinking straight—our veins and arteries are so clogged from eating junk and smoking and drinking booze that oxygen has a hard time reaching our brains, so how is it *possible* to think clearly? After all, our brain is very much like a computer. And when your body is full of tension or in the depths of a depression, you jam your computer, and you can't think clearly.

And the same for your emotions. When you're filled with tension and anxiety, it's impossible to be a loving person. It's not that you don't *want* to be sweet and caring and full of tenderness, you literally *cannot*. When you're tense and anxious, you hit your kids and scream at your husband or wife. You don't want to—you just can't help yourself. And when you're depressed, you're sure not thrilled about hugging and kissing and making nice. You're probably thinking about how you can do away with yourself. So an unhealthy body is not a loving body. But the reverse is certainly true. A *really* healthy body is a loving body.

Sex is a normal function, like eating, drinking, walking, and sleeping. Now you don't feel like eating or drinking when you're sick, and you don't want to walk or move when you're sick, and certainly you don't sleep well when you're sick, and of course you don't want sex when you're sick.

When you're on drugs (cocaine, grass, booze, cigs, coffee, etc.), you can usually eat and drink, though not well. You can usually walk, but not with a bounce in your step, and you can usually sleep, though fitfully. But drugs almost *always* interfere with your sex life.

Sex is one of the best barometers of health that there is. And this goes for both men and women. When a person is a heavy smoker (or even a moderate one), it negatively affects the sex organs. When a man or woman is sexually excited, the sex organs (penis and clitoris) engorge with blood and that's what excites us.

Smoking constricts all the veins and arteries in the body, particularly those in the sex organs, so they can't fill up with blood. This is what we call impotence—a sex organ that won't or can't fill with blood and therefore can't get hard.

And drinking too much booze will deplete the body of all the B vites, which are what keep the nervous system in good shape and keep us relaxed and sensual. So drinking booze will initially make us feel good for a while, and then as the effects wear off, it makes us tense, and we alternate between bouts of depression and anxiety, which feelings are not conducive to love and sex. Indeed, it will chase away any feelings or thoughts you might have had about making love. And coffee will do the same thing. It gives you a temporary "up," then plummets you down, so you need another cup, and another, till your body is so tense and anxious that love and sex are the last things on your mind. And so it goes with all the drugs—cocaine, speed, grass, etc. They're all the same.

Of course, when we smoke or drink too much (women as well as men), it harms lots of *other* parts of our bodies, too, like our lungs, our liver, our heart, our skin, etc., but a *real* barometer of the harm done (and a quicker one) is our sex life. As I said, when we smoke, the nicotine constricts our blood vessels (it really makes them a *lot* smaller), and again, the swelling of the blood vessels is the cause of erection and sexual excitement in both men and women. And the inhaled carbon monoxide reduces the level of blood oxygen as well as hormone production.

When a person is a heavy smoker, the lung capacity is cut *way* down, and that cuts *way* down on your endurance and on the ability to last a while during intercourse. Try it. See what happens when you cut out the smokes for a month. If your sex life doesn't pick up considerably (and I mean your ability as a lover), then you can always go back to smoking. I know it's difficult to stop, but if I did it, anyone can.

Alcoholism is a result of nutritional deficiencies (particularly the B vites), so, because our bodies are malnourished, we crave liquor—which makes our bodies more nutritionally deficient, and we become more malnourished, and we crave more booze, etc., etc., etc.

So the main thing to do for men who want to

have a super sex life is to cut down the booze, cut out the smokes altogether, and start exercising those gorgeous bodies and getting them in shape. Jogging is a terrific way to begin, even if it's running in place in your bedroom. Once you see how good you're feeling, you might even graduate to running outside.

Now I'm sure some men smoke and drink too much and still function well, but believe me, they are the exception. And their sexual prowess won't (can't) last. These men start out in life in better shape than most of us, so it takes the nicotine and booze a little while longer to get to them. But get to them they will.

And as important as it is for *men* to be in great shape physically to be terrific lovers, it's important for women, too. The clitoris is a miniature penis, and if a woman puts gunk in her body, her clit will react exactly the same as a man's penis— it will be difficult, if not impossible, to keep it erect, and she will lose her desire for sex.

Remember, it's *impossible* to keep an erection if your body isn't healthy—it's *not* a mental problem where you can *will* or *demand* your penis to be hard, and it's not an emotional problem where a new and exciting bed partner will stimulate you, and your penis will automatically get hard—it's a *physical* problem if you're mistreating your body by loading it with junk and booze and cigs and other drugs. Your penis *cannot* get hard until you change yourself and get healthy.

Once you get your physical self in great shape, and your mental self sharpens up (which it *will* when your body is activated), and your emotional self softens and expands as the love increases in your life, you'll find the life forces growing greatly in every part of your physical, mental, and emotional self. The ultimate expression of this life force is sex—a juicy, delicious, loving, and exciting sex life. This is only *one* of the ways of pleasuring yourself, but it is the ultimate.

The great turn-on for sex is love, and love is what this book is all about. When you have love radiating from every pore, and love surrounding every thought, and love filling every passion, then you'll know what life is *supposed* to be.

So work at getting healthy, and I promise you you'll feel better than you've ever felt.

I just want to mention something very important to all women re: hormones. I was on birth control (the Pill) for a few years and had no adverse reaction. Then in 1991 I decided to try an in-vitro fertilization. Up till then I had had several miscarriages and had lost a baby (about which I've never been able to speak), so this seemed like a perfect possible solution. I started on extra heavy-duty doses of hormones and felt fine, but sadly lost the embryo baby. I tried it again in 1994, but this time I started to get anxiety attacks right after the hormones. I was determined to continue and said nothing to anyone of the side effects. Then one day in the hospital while the doctor was examining me, I got a very severe physical anxiety attack. My heart was pounding, I was having trouble breathing, and I felt like I was going to die. When the doctor asked me what was wrong I told him, and he said I should have told him this months earlier because I could wear a hormone patch and bypass the stomach, which was where the reaction was taking place.

The patch was great and I continued with it. Unfortunately I lost the second embryo baby after a couple of months, and after this second loss, I started to physically get very anxious and nervous every time I'd put on a patch. I stayed with it but kept asking if there wasn't some thing else to use, and everyone said no, so I didn't know what to do.

Now the reason I'm telling you this is because I discovered a natural estrogen that has absolutely *no* side effects—no nausea, no anxiety, no depression—and I want every woman to at least be aware of it. One day I read Dr. Julian Whittaker's great newsletter, *Health and Healing,* and in it he wrote about a natural estrogen that's so much healthier to use.

It's called C-TRI-EST and it's 80 percent estriol, 10 percent estradiol and 10 percent estrone. Estriol is the safest of all three forms of estrogen in a woman's body, and according to Dr. Whittaker, "it does *not* stimulate cancerous changes in the breast. In fact, it actually *prevents* them." I immediately called my pharmacist, who knew about it but said it's handmade per order and he didn't know who made it. My gynecologist told me to call the Apthorp Pharmacy on the Upper West Side of New York, and sure enough, they made it for me and delivered it. It's more expensive but certainly worth it. I feel so much better, and it's so great to have absolutely *no* side effects and feel so well. With natural versus artificial, natural wins out 100 percent.

And speaking of anxiety, people are so used to feeling tense and anxious that they think it's a natural way of life—that that's the way they're *supposed* to feel. Only after they've gotten rid of tension and anxiety do they realize how awful they *used* to feel and how unnatural it is to feel that awful.

The natural way to feel is calm and relaxed yet full of energy, waking up in the morning wanting to take over the world. That's what life is *supposed* to be like. But most people don't feel that good, and I sure didn't either. I used to be so full of tension and anxiety that I couldn't function, then I'd fall into the pits of depression. I used to think my fears and depressions were all mental, so I tried everything—yoga, psychologists, psychiatrists, meditation—but let me tell you, you can meditate for ten months, or see a shrink for six years, and if your body's screaming out with tension, nothing mental is going to help.

On the other hand, when your body is feeling

super-good, you'll start thinking more clearly than you ever did before—you'll find you don't get confused anymore. And you'll be amazed at how your personal relationships will improve. People will find you more relaxed and more loving—because when you're relaxed and more loving you won't yell at your kids, kick the furniture, or pick fights with your mate.

So the very next step is to get rid of all the physical tension in your body, and I've found the all-time best way to do this. Only a person who's felt as low and really awful as I used to feel can understand why I'm so grateful for the great change that happened to me a few years ago. Anything that could change my life so drastically, that could make me feel so incredibly good every day, is a miracle. If through my experience I can help even one person to feel better, that will make me very happy.

I used to be a wreck on my ten cups (at least) of coffee, my pack a day (at least) of cigarettes, and so many sweets I can't believe I was even alive, let alone functioning. I was tense and anxious between my bouts of depression. Every day I smoked and drank coffee and colas and ate candy and cakes to whip myself into action. Then I'd have a martini to relax at the end of the day, then coffee, cigs, and sweets after dinner to push myself again, and then to bed where I slept horribly, with lots of nightmares, and the next day the same routine all over again.

Finally, at a very young age I had a physical collapse—my body just conked out. I was working at Paramount Studios in Hollywood doing a lead in *Bonanza* ("Ah played Big Red"), and the very last day of filming I couldn't get out of bed to go to the studio. They took me to the hospital, where the doctors thought I had mono or a kidney disease. While I was in the hospital, a friend, Rachel Perry, (the cosmetic queen), gave me one of Adelle Davis's books, and I found out that all the things I'd had wrong with me physically since I was a little kid came from tension, which was caused by a lack of the B vitamins. I later found out that the B vites in my body were being used up by all the sugar and junk I was eating. Sugar has to be metabolized, and it burns up all the B vites in the metabolic process. No wonder I was such a wreck!

Then I found out that nutritional yeast is the

most concentrated source of all the B vites in any food, and those B vites could also knock out tension and depression—so that's when I invented my Dynamite Energy Shake. Not only did the canker sores and neuralgia attacks and pimples go away, but the tension just sort of drained out of my body, and my depressions faded away. I could feel them leaving and a wonderful sense of well-being taking over.

At that time you had to make it from scratch, but now you can buy it ready-made at all health stores, or you can order direct. (You'll find ordering information on page 155.) I worked months perfecting the formula (and I took out the terrible-tasting yeast) so that it would not only make me feel sensational, but would also taste terrific in vanilla, chocolate, strawberry, banana, orange, and maple. You make it with any kind of fruit juice or cold ice water, it tastes great, and all the vites and mins will make you feel super-good. I want *everybody* to feel as good as I do.

I'm so grateful that God gave me my physical collapse that led to my inventing the Dynamite Energy Shake that I decided to put all the money that would have come to me from the sale of the Dynamite Energy Shake, every penny, into a foundation—The John Ellsworth Hayden Foundation—that I named after my late father. The foundation is giving free Dynamite Energy Shakes to every prison I can get it into, because I truly believe that some people commit crimes because of nutritional deficiencies that lead to tension. The same way people drink to escape tension and some fight with their mates and kids and friends as a result of tension, some other people who have chemically imbalanced bodies and serious nutritional deficiencies commit crimes because of the tension.

Free Dynamite Energy Shakes are also going to those people in mental institutes, senior citizens' homes, youth centers, and other places where there are people who I feel could benefit enormously by putting something this potent in their bodies, something that could change their physical, mental, and emotional lives.

In my earlier book, *GOOD IS ALIVE AND WELL AND LIVING IN EACH ONE OF US,* I explain how I became an Honorary Fellow of the International Academy of Preventive Medicine and how I gave testimony in Washington, D.C., at the Congressional Hearings on Nutrition. I also go into the real basics about vitamins, but I'd like to tell you now just a little about why you need them and how many you should take. I've made it *really* logical and simple and easy to understand. I also explain in *HOW TO SATISFY A MAN EVERY TIME* . . . about all the powerful herbs I take besides the amount of vites and mins we should all get every day.

Before I found out about vitamins, I was as confused as everybody else about how many to take and which ones I needed. I used to take a multivitamin once a day, and thought I wasn't getting everything I needed, but now that I've studied and found out a lot about vites, I know I wasn't getting anywhere *near* as many as I needed. It was a joke!

Every body is individual and has individual needs. We don't all need the same amount of vites. What I've done is list what I believe is the *minimum* for *every body* (I take much more, which I list separately). Some of you may need just the minimum, and others may need more like I do.

The bottom line is how do you feel?

List of Vitamins and Minerals*

Vites & Mins	I take 4 tablespoons Dynamite Energy Shake®	I take 6 tablets Dynamite vites®	
Vitamin A (Beta-carotene)	—	15,000 I.U.	
Thiamine (Vitamin B_1)	25 mg	75 mg	
Riboflavin (Vitamin B_2)	25 mg	75 mg	
Niacin (Vitamin B_3)	125 mg	125 mg	
Niacinamide (Vitamin B_3)	125 mg	125 mg	
Calcium	1,000 mg	1,000 mg	
Iron	25 mg	18 mg	
Vitamin B_6	25 mg	75 mg	
Folic acid	400 mcg	400 mcg	
Vitamin B_{12}	100 mcg	100 mcg	
Iodine	210 mcg	150 mcg	
Magnesium	560 mg	400 mg	
Zinc	50 mg	15 mg	
Copper	2 mg	2 mg	
Biotin	300 mcg	300 mcg	
Pantothenic acid	100 mg	150 mg	
PABA	100 mg	150 mg	
Choline	1,000 mg	500 mg	
Inositol	1,000 mg	500 mg	
Potassium	1,000 mg	99 mg	
Papain	100 mg	100 mg	
Selenium	100 mcg	100 mcg	
Ribonucleic acid	100 mg	100 mg	
Betaine	100 mg	100 mg	
Molybdenum	100 mcg	–	
Chromium	100 mcg	100 mcg	
Vanadium	100 mcg	–	
Manganese	3 mg	5 mg	
Vitamin C	—	1,500 mg	(I take 10,000 mg extra)
Vitamin D	—	1,500 I.U.	
Vitamin E	—	200 I.U.	(I take 1,600 units extra)
Phosphorus	—	100 mg	
Citrus bioflavanoids	—	50 mg	
Glutamic acid	—	100 mg	

*Give children proportionately less according to their body weight. For instance, a twelve year old who weighs 100 lbs, give 3/4 of amounts listed, a five year old who weighs 50 lbs, give 1/4 of amounts listed, etc. Give Vit. C according to frequency of colds, etc. the child gets.

Let's start with vitamin A and beta-carotene, which is a non-toxic precursor to vitamin A. That means that the body makes vitamin A from beta-carotene, which is a natural substance. Vitamin A is essential to good skin—it prevents and clears up skin infections. It also makes hair shiny, improves day vision and particularly night vision, promotes cell growth, and aids in resisting infections.

Vitamin A and vitamin E work together and should be taken together, because without vitamin E, vitamin A is destroyed by oxygen. Vitamin A is found in green and yellow vegetables and apricots. The National Research Council recommends 5,000 units a day, but I take much more a day, and I believe that 25,000 units a day should be a minimum for an adult.

The B vitamins are Bl, B2, B6, B12, biotin, folic acid, inositol, niacin, pantothenic acid, and PABA (para-aminobenzoic acid). Science is finding there are other B vites, and has recently isolated two more: Bl6 (pangamic acid) and Bl7 (amygdalin). All the B vites are water soluble and can't be stored in the body, so they must be taken every day. They are synergistic, which means that one alone or several together increase the need for the rest of them. For instance, if you took lots of B_1 or B6, it could make you terribly deficient in all the other Bs. When you take the Dynamite Energy Shake, you'll be getting *all* the B vites, and lots of them, because it's *loaded* with them.

Vitamin C is ascorbic acid, and Nobel Prize winner Linus Pauling recommends at least 3,000 mgs a day, but I take a minimum of 15,000 mgs a day and have for years. If I start to sneeze or feel a cold coming on, I go up to 50,000 mgs a day, and several times I have taken as much as 100,000 mgs in a day, but each time I knocked the virus out that same day, and I can honestly say that since I've been on high doses of vitamin C, *I haven't been sick even one day* (and I used to get colds and flu bugs and viruses maybe eight or ten times a year, bedding me each time for a couple of days—and my doctor bills and antibiotic bills were enormous).

Vitamin C is fantastic, but you do need massive doses (always taken with a *lot* of liquid). *If you're taking vitamin C and still get a cold, then know that you're not taking enough.* And continue taking the large amount of C for at least a day after you start to feel you're all better (and you generally *do* start to feel better right away after taking a lot of C), because if you stop too soon, the germs will begin to multiply again.

If you have bleeding gums or bruises on your body, these are signs of a vitamin C deficiency. If you never get a cold or flu bug, then you probably need far less than the rest of us, and 3,000 or 4,000 mgs a day should be enough for you. Vitamin C is water soluble and can't be stored in the body, so any excess is flushed out, and the body tissues should be saturated with it every day.

Again, be sure to drink lots of liquids when you take lots of vitamin C. Just use your body as a barometer: If you feel great and don't catch colds or viruses, then 3,000 mg a day is enough—if you do catch colds, etc., then you need more.

I drink a lot of water and I can't stress enough how important it is to keep your body hydrated. (I go into great detail in my *GOOD* book about why water is the *most* important thing you can put in your body every day.) Caffeine is a dehydrator, so if you drink anything with caffeine, you need even more water. I drink nothing *but* water; minimally I down at least twelve glasses a day, but usually closer to sixteen, and I feel GREAT!

Vitamin D is known as the sunshine vitamin and helps the body absorb calcium and retain it. Without vitamin D, much calcium is lost. Foods don't contain much, so many people are terribly deficient and don't know why they are so nervous.

Vitamin D cannot be absorbed without fat or oil, so take it after a meal that includes some oil. Vitamin D, like vitamin A (but not beta-carotene), can be toxic, but only in massive doses (over 500,000 units a day). And remember, beta-carotene is a *nontoxic* form of vitamin A. I take two of my own vitamins after each meal, which give me 1,500 units of vitamin D, or 10,500 units a week. Dr. J. A. Johnson of Henry Ford Hospital in Detroit researched vitamin D, and his studies show that an adult can profit by taking at least 4,000 units daily, and even though I take only 1,500 units a day in my vitamins, I get more in the vegetable oil and egg yolks I eat. Of course, I also try to get a *little* sunshine every day just walking around.

Vitamin E helps all the muscles in the body by lowering the need for oxygen. With more oxygen, the heart doesn't have to work as hard. Vitamin E is sometimes called the sex vitamin and helps produce normal sex hormones. Vitamin E also adds oxygen to the brain and has been used to help mentally retarded children. Dr. Del Giudice, head of child psychology at the National Institute of Public Health in Buenos Aires, Argentina, has given mentally retarded children 2,000 to 3,000 units of vitamin E daily for many years with surprisingly successful results and no evidence of toxicity. If you have high blood pressure, I suggest you start very slowly with 100 units of vitamin E, and after you've been on the shake and vites and have gotten healthier and your blood pressure has lowered, then up your vitamin E to 400 units. Most everyone else should begin with 800 units, or if you want to start slowly, 400 units and build up to 800. I take 2,400 units a day now and feel great.

Dolomite contains calcium and magnesium, both super important for your nerves. It comes in pills and powder. A teaspoon of powder in juice or even water (it's tasteless) is equivalent to about ten pills, and ten pills is about the equivalent of the calcium in a quart of milk. If you're under a lot of stress (and who isn't nowadays?), take at least ten pills a day (or one teaspoon of the powder in liquid). I usually take at least ten pills a day, but with all the things I'm doing, I really need 'em to keep me cool. Dolomite is a great natural tranquilizer. It's also awfully important for older people who usually don't get enough calcium and whose bones are getting brittle and porous. It will not only strengthen your bones and keep them from breaking, it'll also calm those frazzled nerves.

I've been taking dolomite for over twenty-five years, so I'm getting calcium not only in my Dynamite but also in these pills, and I've now come out with "Dolomints," which is a minty dolomite. I carry them in my pocket and whenever some little (or big) stress hits, I chew on my Dolomint and in seconds I'm calmed down. See pages 111 and 155 for more info on these Dolomints.

To me one of the saddest and most ridiculous things about MDRs (minimum daily requirements) put out by Washington and used by countless doctors all over the country is the MDR for vitamin C, which is 60 mgs. According to medical statistics 60 mgs of vitamin C will keep you from getting scurvy, which disease marks the last stage of a vitamin C deficiency before you *die*! That's like saying the MDR of water is two ounces a day, which will keep you from dying from a lack of water (or dehydration). Now, obviously one wants to be healthier than a borderline case of scurvy which is one step from death, and the sad part is that so many people accept the MDRs as gospel and are starving their poor bodies from a lack of vitamins, and so many ignorant doctors promote the MDRs as the last word on nutrition. There are lots of great doctors in the world, and there are lots of closed-minded ones. If you're wise, you'll search out the ones who are open minded, who are constantly learning about new findings, and who are into preventive medicine and nutrition.

Just try to remember that vitamins are foods, not drugs. It always astounds me how some doctors warn people about taking vitamins, which are foods and promote great health, and they don't warn people about drinking coffee or colas or eating sugar, all of which are addictive. Once you become aware of your body and listen to what it's telling you, you'll become more sensitive to what it needs, and what to put in and what to keep out. And once you *do* get to know yourself physically and your body starts to feel really healthy, you'll begin to know yourself mentally and emotionally, too. That's the basis of happiness, because when you *really* know yourself, you can get rid of all the negative things and cultivate all the positive things. That's when you'll begin to like yourself, and life will begin to be fun and exciting.

The shakes and vites are not a diet—they're a way of life. They become as much a habit as brushing your teeth every day. Every non-nutritious thing you put in your body is a cause and will have an effect—some right away, like pimples, headaches, canker sores—and some are long-term effects, like strokes, ulcers, and heart attacks. When you abuse your gorgeous body (well, it *will* be when you take care of it), you really can't blame it when it starts to fall apart. But the wonderful thing is that *it's never too late to change.* So even if you've been doing wrong things for years, you can now start a new way of life, one that will make you healthier and happier.

The Dynamite Energy Shake and vites changed my life completely. Now I'm the healthiest, most energetic person I know, and I want *everybody* to feel as good as I do!

8
Living Alone

The ultimate turn-on is love. And when you and your beloved find each other, heaven on earth enters your life.

But what do you do about sex if you're living alone? Your husband died several years ago. Your fella is in the service overseas and won't be back for another year. Your fiancée has dumped you. You decided you would be better off divorced, so you and husby split several months ago.

All right, now you're alone and whether you like it or not is irrelevant. You're trying to make the best of it and you're coping pretty well. Except for sex—or the lack of it. When you had a partner, a mate, you may have fought like crazy, but you were at least with another warm-blooded human being. Because the relationship was so strained, there wasn't a lot of love floating around, but at least there was occasional sex. And as they say, at its worst it's better than anything else.

Self-pleasure is good. *Anything* that gives pleasure, and is healthful and hurts no one including ourselves, is good.

So why is something so good reviled by so many? Because it's not understood and it's cloaked in ignorance and guilt. Most people accept a man's self-pleasure without any problems, so I'm really slanting this to women's pleasure.

Would *anyone* think wrongly of a really hungry person going into a well-stocked kitchen, looking at all the edibles, choosing a plate of steaming pasta primavera, and sitting down and slowly eating every last bite? Obviously not.

Then why would anyone want to deprive himself or herself or anyone else of another need that is just as important? If you don't eat food for a long enough period of time, your body will die. You need good healthful nourishment to thrive. And if you don't have an orgasm for a long period of time, your body will get very tense, your blood pressure will go up, you will not feel really good, and you will definitely get depressed. And the instinctive physical way to get rid of depression is anger.

So when you see an habitually angry and tense person, know that that person hardly ever or never has an orgasm. Those substances called endorphins, which give you a sense of well being when they're released in your body via an orgasm, will be withheld, and you will get more tense, more depressed, and more difficult to be around. (Endorphins are also released through exercise, which is a *great reason to stay in shape*.)

All those awful sexist stories about a cranky female needing an orgasm are true, but they are equally true for a cranky male. Except if a man went months or years without an orgasm, he'd be *worse* than cranky, he'd be violent!

Think about *that* with all the violence in the world.

If a woman is married and her sexually ignorant husband doesn't know how to intercourse correctly, and she, just as ignorant, doesn't know what to tell him to do to give her an orgasm, you've got a tense and unhappy wife. And if she's single and alone (and tense and unhappy), her own ignorance about self-pleasure is obvious.

And all older men and women who think that sex is now unimportant for them should know that part of the reason for their depression is that their bodies haven't lost their need for the now-missing endorphins. They may think it has, their minds may be telling them that sex is only for the young, but almost *all* older people who are active and not depressed, tense and/or angry, are getting sexual pleasure, either with a spouse or alone. Of course they don't talk about it, but I've interviewed many seniors who do, and many who don't, and it's the happy, non-angry, non-tense ones who do.

One woman's terminally ill husband made her promise that she would pleasure herself after he was gone. She told me he was extremely loving all their forty-two years of marriage—he *always* wanted her to have sexual pleasure, and he *always* made sure she did.

Sex is a part of nature. Our sex drive is a physical need just as our hunger drive is. We didn't *ask* for our sex organs, but they're part of the package. And to ignore them isn't just ignorant, it's stupid.

When a single woman learns about self-pleasure and sensualizes with it, her compulsive need to be with a man (whether he's good for her or not) leaves her, and she can wait for sex till she meets the right compatible man and falls in love with him. This makes her more self-reliant and a happier person.

Any time you can rely on yourself, you're going to be happier. Dependence on others can be a mirage—when you really need them the most, that's when they're usually not there.

But your self is *always* there. So nurture your body with really good nutritious foods, drink lots of water, get plenty of rest and sleep, and pleasure yourself as often as you want so that you'll always feel good.

In his book *Sex Can Save Your Heart and Life,* Dr. Eugene Scheimann points out that celibacy just about destroyed earlier civilizations and that some scholars believe that celibacy, not orgies, led to the decline and fall of the Roman Empire:

"During the early centuries, the Christians actually tried to get rid of sex entirely. . . . It wasn't Christ's idea, nor that of his earliest followers with the possible exception of Saint Paul, but his later followers became obsessed with stamping out sex. . . . Over the years, this attitude took its toll. The glorification of celibacy led to a decline in the population of the Western Empire. The defeat of Rome by the barbarian Huns from the north has been blamed on everything from decadence to lead poisoning, but one scholar, Dr. Richard Lewinsohn, claims that the antisex doctrine was responsible. "Unless we can assume that the innumerable treatises in favor of asceticism were mere literary efforts and that no one except a few thousand monks and nuns ordered their lives after them, one is forced to conclude that sexual abstinence did more [than corruptionl to bring about the downfall of Rome."

Again, sex is a natural function just like eating, drinking, walking, and sleeping. Just as you hopefully don't glut your body by gorging with food or drink till your belly juts out, you also hopefully don't starve your body of nutrients, or keep yourself from drinking liquids till you're all shriveled from thirst.

All appetites are meant to be satisfied. Not gorged and not starved. A happy medium. We use self-control. Someone may give you a gorgeous chocolate mousse cake, but that doesn't mean you dive in and eat the whole thing in one sitting. That would undoubtedly make you sick. A small slice after dinner, another small slice tomorrow. With care, it could last a week or two.

The same with sex. It's certainly all around us, and it's not too difficult to come by nowadays. But just to grab the first available body is not the answer. In fact, that will probably disgust yourself with yourself and could turn you off sex *altogether* for a while.

Now, if you're a healthy person, you're going to have a healthy sex drive. You didn't ask for it. You were born with it. *All* healthy persons have healthy sex drives. It makes no difference if you're a priest, nun, schoolteacher, postman, race-car driver, movie star, astronaut, or attorney. If you're healthy, it's there. Some of us may try to sublimate it in religious activities or sports or an artistic endeavor. But it's still there. And wishing won't make it go away.

Again, Dr. Eugene Scheimann says:

"Freud was not the first doctor to notice that people who got sick often had severe sex problems. But Freud was the first to make this a subject for science. . . . His theories became the basis of psychiatry, and the foundation of psychosomatic medicine. . . . he demonstrated that when sexual desires are repressed into the unconscious, they often show up, not only in dreams and accidents and psychological upsets, but in organic disease. . . . Recent insights into human sexuality seem to suggest that not only was he on the right track, but that in truth he didn't go far enough."

So what to do without a partner? Well, there are pros and cons to self-satisfaction. Michael, a character in Mart Crowley's Off-Broadway play *The Boys in the Band,* believes it cuts down your wardrobe needs. He says, "Well, one thing you can say for masturbation—you certainly don't have to look your best."

Some people believe in it and do it all the time, and others are offended by the mere mention of it. I personally think that anything in life that doesn't hurt you in any way physically, mentally, or emotionally, or doesn't hurt anyone else physically, mentally, or emotionally, and is pleasure-full and feels good and is healthful and is good for your circulation and well-being *must* be good.

But if you feel that something—*anything*—is not good for you, and that thing—whatever it is—makes you feel guilty, then I don't think you should do it. This goes for food that you eat, liquids that you drink, actions that you make, and sex.

I believe sex should always be with love, but then I believe that *everything* should be done with love. What is love? It's caring—caring about yourself, your family, your friends, your pets, your plants. And what is caring? Taking care of. So to love is to take care of. When you truly love yourself, you take care of yourself—you take care that you put only healthful foods and healthful drinks into your body, and only healthful thoughts and feelings into your mind. Love is all-pervasive.

And if you're living alone, either through circumstance or through choice, love should be in every part of *your* life, too. You have no one to take care of but yourself, and you have no one to take care of *you* but yourself, so *you* have to care for yourself. Caring is love and love is caring.

You should care for and pleasure yourself in every possible way that makes you feel good physically, mentally, and emotionally.

In the *Redbook* survey is this report:

"The activity once thought to cause warts is now recommended to do all but cure them . . . therapists advise masturbation to survive sexually without a partner."

In *Sexual Confidence,* Dr. Debora Phillips says:

"The list of bad things about masturbation can be summed up in a word: Nothing. Except the attitude that masturbation is shameful.

Masturbation is a pleasure. And human beings are especially endowed with a great capacity for pleasure. The woman's clitoris, for example, has nothing to do with procreation. The only function a clitoris has is to give pleasure. Isn't it remarkable that we humans have been given an organ that is only for sexual pleasure?"

Dr. Phillips goes on:

"The Reverend Dr. William Kirby, a Protestant theologian, states, "Let's start with love. Is sex loving? Sex before or after marriage or between two individuals of the same or different sex cannot simply be placed into a category of good or bad or wrong or right or liberating or confining, but rather whether it is loving."

Then she adds:

"Theologian and author Rabbi Reeve Brenner points out: "To Jews, sex is a blessing. . . . In the Hebrew Bible (the Old Testament) and in the Talmud, Judaism makes a strong argument *against* celibacy and *for* the raptures of love."

If you've found the love of your life and you have a great relationship, you're a lucky person—but if you haven't, don't deny yourself pleasure. Certainly love is the all-time greatest pleasure in the world, but love comes in many packages. I believe in feeling good so long as you don't hurt yourself or anyone else. The only possible thing that could hurt you is guilt, and if you're a loving person who's actively spreading love, there's nothing to be guilty about.

Again, pleasure yourself as much and as often as you can. Eat wholesome food, breathe clean, fresh air, drink lots of pure water, use all your muscles, take good care of your skin and body. Do as many of the things that you can do to make yourself feel better physically, mentally, emotionally and spiritually.

9
The Joy of Marriage

Now we come to my favorite subject, marriage. I don't believe in living together—"playing house"—and I truly believe in the commitment of marriage. I think it's the greatest relationship that two people can ever have. A partnership with someone who loves you. What could be better?

I also believe strongly, as I stated earlier, in faithfulness in marriage. I don't think you can break the bond of trust in a marriage without seriously damaging the relationship. And I don't mean that he'll find out she's fooling around, or she'll catch him with another woman. I mean the person who's *cheating* will feel damaged.

That person will know the trust is broken, and the relationship can never be the same.

I hate it when a married man makes a play for me. Even if he's the handsomest, darlingest man-about-town, it truly distresses me. I don't want him to embarrass his wife by flirting outrageously with me or any other woman.

And I'm *really* happy when a married man is attentive to his wife and acts like he's in love, and doesn't make goo-goo eyes at me or anyone else.

That might seem strange, you might think I would *love* any male attention, but again for Naura's logic. A man who pays attention to his wife, who is polite and gracious but doesn't single out or flirt with other women, proves to me that it is possible to find a man who will be faithful, who won't fool around, and who can be trusted. The married man who ignores his wife and flirts with me would flirt with other women *exactly* the same way if he were married to me.

I want a man who loves me and who is faithful *because* of his love and devotion and trust and all those other beautiful feelings that we all have but don't always use.

So why do so many people fool around outside

of marriage? Why is it thousands and thousands of marriages are broken up every day? Why do families split, destroying children's emotional lives and traumatizing the broken partners?

I believe most of it stems from incomplete sex lives. Most women are faking orgasms and are deeply dissatisfied sexually with their husbands and their marriages, and are looking around for "Mr. Right" to fulfill them in this very important way.

And the men fooling around are doing it because they sense their wives are not *deeply* in love with them, and all men, like all women, are searching for a deep emotional love. *Deep* love comes only when both partners are united heart to-heart, soul-to-soul, and body-to-body.

Now I've heard lots of people say that sex isn't everything, and that it's overstated in a relationship. People have told me that companionship and compatibility are what really count, and that sex isn't that important or necessary for a happy marriage, and also that many marriages are just as happy without it.

I *totally* disagree with this.

To me, being married and living together

without sex is like cooking a super-delectable seven course dinner and saying, "You can look at it, you can touch it, you can smell it, you can taste it, but you *can't* eat it!"

You can be married and compatible and love to do all the same kinds of things together, but without sex, your union is not complete. And anyone who says it is has obviously got problems in his or her sex life, and the marriage can't be a really happy and complete one.

Of *course,* companionship is important in a relationship, very important. And having things in common is what makes you so compatible. The fact that you both love movies and hate picnics, or adore dancing and loathe golf, is part of what makes being together fun. But sex is one of the strongest and most important feelings we have in life—physically, mentally, and emotionally. And to underestimate it is a foolish and dangerous thing to do, because that might lead you to overlook unhappiness in the boudoir, instead of looking for solutions.

Sure, other things are important, but don't ever forget that sex is the *closest* two people can get. Certainly physically (you literally can't *get* any closer!), but also there is a bond formed mentally and emotionally when sexual pleasuring is the ultimate joy for both partners.

I believe God gave us our sex organs so that we would be bonded to each other in pleasure *forever* within marriage. Sex was also given to us for procreation. But if this were *all* it was for, sexual feelings would then cease when a woman can't procreate, or when a man is unable to have children. And they don't.

If a man and woman are *truly* sexually happy together, there would be no reason for him or her to look elsewhere for sex. When a man and woman love each other and share the joy of ecstasy when they express their love in sex, why *would* they look around?

I want to explain now that what I have to say is *only* for a woman and a man who either now have or at one time had a deep love and need for each other. I consider myself a feminist (I've always supported myself, I believe in equal pay and all *other* equality, I bought my own home, etc.), but some feminists who have never been deeply in love with a man don't understand that sexual surrender is what happens to *both* the husband and the wife, and it's what makes a truly great and successful marriage.

And I also want to say that I believe so deeply in sex with love and commitment that I want to warn you that casual sex can be dangerous. I don't mean the obvious disease danger, but the emotional batterings that can scar you for life when you go from one body to another with no feeling emotionally, or a lot of feeling emotionally that is not reciprocated.

Again, the great pleasure of sex was given to us originally to insure that we procreate, and way down deep, way beyond our conscious mind, that desire to further the species is still with us. Even though we use the Pill and condoms and other birth-control methods, way back in the recesses of our beings is the need to create another human being with a caring partner. And because we *do* have feelings, to have endless affairs without love or caring isn't fair to you or your affair partner.

What every one of us is looking for—and what will make each one of us happy—is to find that one person with whom we're compatible, that one person who shares our likes and dislikes, and to also share a loving, monogamous, sexual relationship with that one person.

A truly sad story I read a few years ago was told by a woman doctor in her eighties who had been very happily married right after the turn of the century. She was deeply in love with her husband, another doctor, who loved her just as deeply. She told how one night at the beginning of their marriage they made love and she experienced the most incredible feeling of ecstasy that she had ever felt, a feeling of her body exploding and expanding into space. Much later, she learned that what she had experienced was an orgasm. At that time, however, the ecstasy of the feeling was *so* intense that it frightened her and her husband to the extent that in later sex relations she tensed up physically to keep herself from any further enjoyment of her husband's body-union with her. They were both taught that a woman did not enjoy sex, that any pleasure in the sex act was forbidden for a woman.

She related how he died a few years later, and when she finally realized that her ecstasy with her mate was a beautiful and tender part of their love, something to be cherished, not feared, and that she had stopped it—she had actually *killed* all the physical joy and passion with the man she totally loved—her regret was so profound that it filled her with a sadness that she could never shake for the rest of her life.

How lucky we are today to be living in an era of openness in so many areas. Men and women today are frank in their discussions of sex. Years ago, when there was so much shame and guilt, no *wonder* THE BIG BANG got started. Wham, bam, thank you ma'am. Just do it fast and hard and get it over with No wonder women (and men) have had so many sexual problems through the years. Shame and guilt are *awful* bedfellows.

A great part of great love, a very, *very* important part, is expressing that love through sex.

A few years ago I created a phrase: "Pay attention instead of alimony."

Alimony is expensive (for men *and* women!). Attention isn't.

Attention is a pat on the fanny, a "you look great!", and even a simple "I love you," and if you have trouble saying *that*, say "Isle of View" (from the book of the same name)!

Attention is taking your spouse's hand while walking down the street, winking across a crowded cocktail party, calling long distance the night you arrive across the country and saying "I just wanted you to know I miss you."

Attention is a lot of things. A lot of simple things. But most importantly it's letting your mate know you care. You care how he feels. You care how she looks. You care what he eats and drinks. You care that she keeps healthy.

Caring is loving. Loving is caring.

When you focus your loving attention on *anything,* it will thrive, be it your spouse, your kids, your parents, your employees, your boss, your pals, your animals, your plants—attention is like warming rays of sunshine.

And one of the things to pay attention to is sex. Don't make the mistake of thinking it's not important (as so many women told me when I toured the country with this marriage manual).

It's *always* important to a man (a normal, healthy man), and it *will* be important to every woman when her husband learns how to give her this beautiful, loving pleasure *every time* they make love.

And don't forget yourself. If you don't pay attention to yourself, you really *can't* pay attention to anyone else. If you don't eat right, you won't feel right, and how can you be loving and kind to *anyone* else if you're tense, anxious, depressed, or have pains in your stomach?

So paying attention starts with yourself, spreads to your spouse, kids, parents, and friends, and never ends.

If you truly care enough to pay attention, *real* attention, to listen and respond with care, the rewards are far greater than you might imagine—in fact, you might really be surprised. . . .

The few people I know who have happy relationships *all* pay attention instead of alimony. They have learned that the greatest joy in the whole world is to be deeply loved and cared for and pleasured sexually by your mate.

This is *truly* the joy of marriage.

And the joy of marriage is *truly* the joy of life!

A Married Man's Incredible Letter to Me

I have received tens of thousands of letters since my book came out in 1982, and I cannot tell you how thrilling it is for me to know that my book has saved so many marriages, and made so many other marriages happier than they ever thought possible.

Some are from couples who tell me they were going to marriage counselors, and some of them were cheating on each other, but after using the technique, *all* said they were closer and happier than ever, and now totally monogamous.

Others are from wives telling me they had never had an orgasm before they and their husbands read the book.

Others are from husbands saying they never felt so much love from their wives as now since they learned how to intercourse correctly.

Still others told me they were actually in the process of getting a divorce when the husband or wife got my book, got the spouse to read it, and changed their whole lives around with more emotional intimacy than they ever dreamed possible.

But the most incredible letter I *ever* received arrived in November of 1991 from a man in Virginia who sent me 14 handwritten pages (he says at the end that he obviously couldn't have had his secretary type it), and it is such a sincere and loving letter from a husband who genuinely really loves his wife of 18 years that I was emotionally moved by it.

He tells how upset and frustrated he was by her lack of responsiveness and pleasure in lovemaking during their years together, so much so that he contemplated cheating on her and even thought about the possibility of divorce.

He says my book changed his life and his marriage . . .

11/18/91   7:19 A.M.

Dear Naura :

I've never written to an author before.
I've enjoyed alot of books and some
have moved me, some changed me and
some have taught me something. But I've
never had a book change my life before.
Over this past weekend I was driving my
son (13) to a soccer tournament. He
was asleep in the back of the van and
it was probably 10:30 at night. I
~~found~~ ~~was~~ was trying to find a
radio station to keep ~~me~~ awake. I still
had 100 miles to go. I heard your
interview on your book How To Satisfy a
Woman Every Time   and somehow knew you
were onto something.

My wife and I have been married for
18 years. In that time she has probably
had 18 ~~████~~ orgasms. She never liked
oral sex; (said it tickled too much).
Manual manipulation was OK up to
a point, she'd get excited and want me
to put my penis inside her, NOW!
Over the years I've read all variety
of sex books trying to find a way to
help her achieve orgasm. We ended up
fighting over sex because I felt she
was frigid because of a horrible

relationship with her stepfather.
She has told me how afraid of him
she was — that she was always afraid
to be alone with him because of sexual
comments. I believe he probably sexually
abused her but she has never been able
to admit this, perhaps not even to
herself. He certainly did severe
emotional damage to her and I believed
this was why she was "frigid". In the final
analysis, I felt she was afraid to let herself orgasm.

She and I even went to a sex therapist
(psychologist) for a while but that did no
good. I just wanted her to feel good
sexually & that I could make her feel
good. I'll certainly admit that it was
a real ego blow for me that I couldn't
help my wife achieve orgasm more than once
a year. I know she did reach orgasm once
a year (approximately) because she never
faked it. Her most telling statements
in that time were: "there's nothing
wrong with me, I just don't have
orgasms very often, I just can't relax
enough, you'll just have to accept me
as I am." Those words have rung in
my ears for years and I felt totally
helpless to do anything about it because
she gave up wanting to try.

She hated to talk about sex, and although she promised to read the occasional therapy book I brought home, she never did.

Interestingly she was the one that always hurried sex. Foreplay was very short — she said it tickled too much and just wanted me in her. I don't think it was just to get it over with because foreplay was so short I wasn't sufficiently aroused ~~for the therapy to help quickly~~ for me to come quickly.

It's also important to note that I have been so frustrated by "her" lack of ~~responsiveness~~ that I have ~~contemplated~~ divorce in passing many times believing I would be happier with a "sexually responsive" woman. Sex has become less frequent in recent years because she's too tired, not feeling good, etc. I always have felt that if she could achieve ~~orgasm~~ orgasm more often she would be more interested (Now, I'll get to find out, but more about that later.)

That night on the radio, although you weren't explicit about your technique, your sincerity told me you knew what you were talking about. While driving 70 mph down the highway I managed to write your name, 800 # and

write me, I feel like you're a friend.
If you are doing an appearance in Washington,
D.C. area please let me know, I'd just like
to thank you personally. There's a great
deal more I'd like to say but I think this
letter is longer than ~~your~~ book. Even
if you don't get to read the letter, I feel
better for having written it.

THANK YOU AND LET ME KNOW IF THERE IS
ANYTHING I CAN DO FOR YOU.

If you do write please send it to my company
address marked personal & confidential

thanks ———

PS. Please forgive the hand written, rambling nature of this letter
I couldn't ask my secretary to type it!

two. She thought she wanted ~~that I~~ me to be all the way in and I thought she did too. It's so sad that ~~we~~ allowing us both to give in to that was ~~so~~ self defeating.

Anyway, on to the main event. After the tournament my son & I drove home and I kept running through my mind ~~how~~ I would ~~approach~~ the subject of your book, methods, and get her to read it. We got the kids ~~to bed~~, cleaned up downstairs and went to bed ourselves. As she was changing I told her ~~about~~ your radio interview ~~and~~ that I had read your book and felt you were really onto something, I told her I wanted her to give me ~~the birthday~~ a birthday present. (I'll be 40, next week) I wanted her to read the book. She indicated she would, but once again I could hear in her voice, she had no intention of doing so. I think your book represented a threat. If she read it and we tried your techniques and they didn't work — once again she would have failed. Even though it wouldn't have been a failure on her ~~part~~ I must admit I would have silently blamed her and her background for her failure to achieve orgasm and based on

my blaming her, other ~~books~~ blaming
her (a woman is responsible for her own ~~orgasm~~),
and the sex therapist blaming her, I'm sure
she must have either been blaming herself
or hating the world when it came to ~~the subject~~
or both. That's the other reason woman fake it. They think
something is wrong with them.

forgosm

Anyway, I did not tell her anything about
your techniques but wanted to let her
curiosity to take over. I wasn't sure ~~it would~~
~~work.~~ She would read it regardless.

She then came over to my side of the bed to
cuddle as she frequently does when she wants
to make love. I began running my fingertips
up and down her arm. She began to shiver,
and said, "You know I don't like you to touch
me that lightly, it tickles too much."
I started rubbing her back the same way which
she tolerated for a while but clearly was
uncomfortable. She rolled over onto her back
and put my hand on her ~~still~~ still ~~panty~~ clad
vagina. She ~~apparently~~ figured she needed once
again, to ~~speed~~ this whole thing up. She
didn't want to be "tickled" anymore. ~~Instead,~~
I moved my hand up to her breast and started
making slow light fingertip touch circles
about her nipple. She held my hand with which
I was caressing her ~~with, some~~ as ~~he~~ she always does,
so she can pull my hand away when

she becomes too sensitive. Again, she tolerated the fingertip touch for about a minute, but again I felt the need to speed things up. Because she could see I was in no hurry she pulled her panties off, pushed me onto my back and began to mount me. I felt defeated because as she lowered herself on me it was difficult for me to keep her out, with her on top. _How was I going to get her to read the Book_?

As I lay on my back I put my hands under her hips and kept her from ~~fully~~ being fully penetrated. She was frustrated by this but "tolerated" it for awhile because she knew I was up to something based on your book, she just couldn't figure out what. After a few minutes of this, she decided she'd had enough of this foolishness and pulled me over into the missionary position. NOW, I WAS IN CONTROL!

I pulled back and continually moved my penis into and around the opening of her vagina paying particular attention to the top and her clitoris. Slowly, gently, carefully probing never entering her more than with the head of my penis. We went on like this for 5 to 10 minutes and I could just feel her excitement increasing. Her breathing got deeper and pronounced. A few times she grabbed my hips and tried to pull me all the way in but I resisted her. She tensed and seemed almost angry. I ignored this response and just kept going lightly, right at the rim. Finally, (you're right!) she begged — "please put it in!" And for the first time I said gently but firmly (and with a fair amount of self control) "no! not yet."

Now she understood, I could feel she understood. I was in control of her, and I was not going to enter her until I was ready. She was getting more intense feelings all the time and we were going to continue just this way until I decided to change it. It was marvelous. Based on this new unspoken understanding, I continued to tease her for another few minutes. Then it happened, she tried to pull me in one more time and I wouldn't let her. Then she orgasmed. I hadn't gotten to the ½", 1", 1½", 2" penetration you suggested, I was still teasing at the opening because I didn't want to lose control of the situation, her or myself. I'll have to work on that in the future.

ANYWAY, SHE ORGASMED! I was on cloud nine

She pulled me to her and I went ~~in~~ hungrily but carefully. She bucked and her vagina and love channel ~~spasmed~~ around me in a way I had only felt a few times previously. I came within a minute and felt like a million, no ~~$~~ten million dollars, (after taxes). I HAD DONE IT. That's the funny part. I felt like she had to [have an orgasm herself] ~~do it~~ and ~~I now know~~ know something incredibly powerful. I can completely control her body. What an incredible turn-on. I have the capability to drive the woman I love completely out of her mind. She could always do it to and for me but I could never do it to or for her. Boy, I sure can now.

My orgasm was incredibly intense because I knew I had given her ~~one~~ an orgasm and while I was teasing her, I was teasing myself too.

I now want to go back and re-read how to give her multiple orgasms. She's never done that before & I bet I can help her do that too. Frankly, I want to achieve that because I have a ~~rather~~ voracious sexual appetite with the ability to come three times in an hour. If I can get her turned on rather than hurt and frustrated—hopefully

she'll want to make love so that I can
come more than once **in** a session.

~~XXXXXXXX~~

She fell asleep afterward holding my hand. I can't
remember that ever happening and you can't believe
how good that felt to me.

NOW, — how have you changed my life.

① I can't tell for sure yet in all the sexual
aspects but if you write me a note and
tell me you're interested I'll write you
again in 6 months ~~if you write me~~
if ~~fuck and tell~~ me you'd like to hear more.
I'll tell you how we're doing in bed

② ~~As I say~~
I believe you've saved my marriage.
I LOVE MY WIFE. She's bright, articulate,
attractive, a wonderful mother for our 3 kids,
and she's my best friend. We've always been
able to talk about anything openly and honestly
except for sex. Our marriage has been
a beautiful cooperative partnership,
except for sex. (She's a candidate for a
Ph.D. and will receive it in the Spring of
'92.) The kids and I have supported her
through all of that.
A long time ago I realized I loved this woma

deeply and although our sex life was lousy — everything else was too good to give up. I tried to "live" with it. My male ego was hurt badly and I was increasingly tempted to seek out a "responsive bed partner" to fill that void. I was even thinking that cheating would help keep my marriage together. The saddest part is that if I had decided to cheat and found a good "faker" I might have eventually left my wife.

<u>What a stupid and dangerous game.</u>

From an: emotional standpoint

getting caught standpoint

<u>disease</u> standpoint ——> and family

hurting and losing my wife standpoint.

<u>But I was feeling that desparate.</u> I thought
it was the only way to keep my marriage together.
I was so emotionally hurt it was the only
way I saw I could fill the void.

<u>I DON'T NEED TO DO THAT ANYMORE.</u>

My mental state is wonderful this morning.

③ I quit smoking this morning. I now want
to live a long life with my wife &
have every reason to live. I was
smoking and drinking too much). It was
clearly stifling my sex drive some — not
alot. Since we were down to having
sex three times a week (I was still
masturbating 7 times a week) it helped
some but it was also killing me. I now
know I will be able to get both out
of my life. (smoking & drinking)
I am happier than I have been in a long time.

Finally, perhaps I can do something for you. When you're on a talk show in the future I'd sure like to know. I'd love to call in and tell people the importance of your book. You are an incredible woman. I can only grieve for ⸺ my first 18 years of marriage based on my ignorance.

Use any of this letter that will help you promote the book. I'm going to sign my name to this letter because I want you to know every word is true — although I suspect you already know that it is. Please don't use my name, not because it would bother me but because it would hurt my wife.

I only wish the book could be given to every couple that applies for a marriage license. I don't know how much the divorce rate would be reduced but I believe it would reduce it some. Some percentage of couples get divorced because of sexual incompatibility and Betty and I could have ended up that way. YOU'VE CHANGED MY LIFE!

I sincerely hope that you get a chance to

write me, I feel like you're a friend. If you are doing an appearance in Washington, D.C. area please let me know, I'd just like to thank you personally. There's a great deal more I'd like to say but I think this letter is longer than your book. Even if you don't get to read the letter, I feel better for having written it.

THANK YOU AND LET ME KNOW IF THERE IS ANYTHING I CAN DO FOR YOU.

If you do write please send it to my company address marked personal & confidential

thanks —

PS. Please forgive the hand written, rambling nature of this letter. I couldn't ask my secretary to type it!

Afterword

To all you men out there who are putting into action what you've just read, and are no longer practicing THE BIG BANG THEORY, but are, with much love, gently and tenderly pleasuring your women . . .

thank you . . .

And to all you women no longer faking it, but enjoying sex completely, with warm feelings and open hearts, who are with much love and passion pleasuring your men . . .

thank you . . .

Because from all of you who are giving and receiving and making love, lots of that love is spilling over and touching all the rest of us, and because we're all connected, when you're more loving it touches me, and when I'm more loving it touches you.

We're all in this together, and love makes us know we're all one.

NLAURA'S OTHER BOOKS

HOW TO SATISFY A <u>MAN</u> EVERY TIME . . . and have him beg for more!
- A marriage manual and a marriage saver!
- This is the first and *only* book that shows a woman *exactly* how!

Hardcover $15.95

Everything You've Always Wanted to Know about ENERGY . . . But Were Too Weak to Ask
- All about physical, mental, and emotional energy
- Over 2 million copy best-seller
- On every best-seller list in the country
- "Naura's energy is contagious. This book can make us all superstars."—Dr. Robert Atkins

Hardcover $19.95

Isle of View (Say It Out Loud!)
- This book full of love energy will change your life!
- "This upbeat book follows its predecessor onto the best-seller lists."—*Publishers Weekly*

Hardcover $19.95

Astro-Logical Love
- *A logical* look at astrology!
- Do the simple charts in just minutes and find out about personality and character traits of yourself, your love, your ex-love, your future love, your children, friends, enemies, employer, employees, etc.

- "Do a chart and find out about everyone you know."—*People*

Hardcover $21.95

The Hip, High-Prote, Low-Cal, Easy-Does-lt Cook book
- *A* vegetarian cookbook with over two hundred delicious meatless recipes

"Heartily recommended . . . the buy of the year."
  —*King Features*

Hardcover $19.95

GO*O*D IS ALIVE AND WELL AND LIVING IN EACH ONE OF US

- *A* revolutionary self-change book for physical, mental, emotional, and spiritual growth

Hardcover $21.95

On sale at all bookstores.

To order direct, using any major credit card, call 1-800-255-1660, M—F, 9:30-5:30 EST.

Or send check or money order to: Suite 2C, 200 West 58th Street, New York, NY 10019. Enclose $5.00 for each hard cover for postage and handling.

To order Naura's DYNAMITE ENERGY SHAKE, DYNAMITE VITES, or DOLOMINTS, call 1-800-255-1660, M-F, 9:30-5:30 EST.

Naura's Web site: www.naura.com.